The Politics of Penance

The Politics of Penance

Proposing an Ethic for Social Repair

Michael Griffin

Foreword by
Daniel Philpott

 CASCADE *Books* · Eugene, Oregon

THE POLITICS OF PENANCE
Proposing an Ethic for Social Repair

Cascade Books
An Imprint of Wipf and Stock Publishers
199 W. 8th Ave., Suite 3
Eugene, OR 97401

www.wipfandstock.com

PAPERBACK ISBN: 978-1-4982-0424-8
HARDCOVER ISBN: 978-1-4982-0426-2
EBOOK ISBN: 978-1-4982-0425-5

Cataloguing-in-Publication data:

Names: Griffin, Michael. | Philpott, Daniel, 1967–, foreword.

Title: The politics of penance : proposing an ethic for social repair / Michael Griffin ; foreword by Daniel Philpott.

Description: Eugene, OR : Cascade Books, 2016 | Includes bibliographical references.

Identifiers: ISBN 978-1-4982-0424-8 (paperback) | ISBN 978-1-4982-0426-2 (hardcover) | ISBN 978-1-4982-0425-5 (ebook)

Subjects: LSCH: Penance. | Reparation (Criminal justice). | Responsibility. | Restitution. | Reconciliation.

Classification: BJ1451 .G74 2016 (print) | BJ1451 .G74 (ebook)

Manufactured in the U.S.A.   07/26/16

Contents

Foreword

IRISH MONKS, CONTEMPORARY PERU, passages from Thomas Aquinas, Pope John Paul II's mea culpas, and penitential rites: How can such seemingly disparate fragments occupy the same text, as they do in the pages that follow? Such is the Christian tradition, where concepts, practices, and teachings that previous communities long ago left in the ruins later become disinterred, revived through divine breath, and deployed into new circumstances.

The new circumstances for which Dr. Michael Griffin retrieves and threads together these discarded shards are the manifold contemporary contexts in which past injustices have inflicted great wounds on social orders. Yes, *social* orders. Until recently, Christian ethics has had strikingly little to say about how to repair social fabrics that have been rent apart by yesterday's injustices—sometimes atrocious injustices. Sin, forgiveness, penance, and satisfaction, to the degree that these themes have received emphasis at all, were relegated to the confession booth (in the Catholic tradition) or individual consciences (as Protestants would have it). Ethics, on the other hand, has been about what people and institutions ought or ought not to do—abortion, economic justice, immigration, and so on.

If, however, the first half of the twentieth century did not make it clear that facing past injustices is a rich and complex matter of ethics, the second half of that century and the first part of the current century have left no doubt about the matter whatsoever. Not only have genocides and civil wars continued to unfold in Yugoslavia, Rwanda, Sudan, and Peru, but also, remarkably, a wave of efforts to address these atrocities has arisen. We have seen more than forty truth commissions, international and national tribunals, reparations schemes, the rise of political apologies, the emergence of forgiveness in politics, memorials, monuments, civil society reconciliation initiatives, and scores of other measures for addressing the past. To these contemporary social evils and emergent remedies, Dr. Griffin appropriately adds the appalling incarceration crisis in the United States and creatively incorporates the struggles of veterans returning from war in Iraq and Afghanistan. How shall we address the wounds of those who suffered these injustices? And even more interestingly, how shall we address those who perpetrated them?

This is where Dr. Griffin takes up his work of retrieval. The Irish monks, Thomas Aquinas, and John Paul II become his companions as he seeks to show that addressing past sin—confronting, exposing, defeating, healing—is a social affair, and that when it is recognized as such, practices like penance, satisfaction, restitution, and reparation can be marshaled to great restorative effect. Not only will the Christian tradition be thus renewed, but so can modern political orders, criminal justice systems, and the task of reintegrating veterans.

Dr. Griffin is just the scholar for this task of retrieval. His life has led him to it. Inspired by the radical social vision and nonviolent witness of the Catholic Worker community, he was then led to accompany returning veterans through the Catholic Peace Fellowship. His vision of peace was thus deepened into one of repair. Through his doctoral studies—a part of which was a study of recently emergent Christian writings on political reconciliation that we conducted together—he expanded this vision of repair to a theological one with applications to a wider set of social contexts. The result lies in the pages that follow. Herein, I am confident, lies a key contribution to a critically important development in the Christian tradition.

—Daniel Philpott

Professor of Political Science and Peace Studies,
Director of the Center for Civil and Human Rights,
University of Notre Dame
December 31, 2014

Acknowledgments

I WOULD LIKE TO thank my closest mentors over the years at Notre Dame, in particular those who guided my doctoral work: Todd Whitmore, Margie Pfeil, and Dan Philpott. Special thanks also go to Tim Matovina, who has been a constant source of encouragement. I am grateful to my colleagues at Holy Cross College, who have advanced my scholarship during my time here, especially Bill Mangan, Justin Watson, Br. John Paige, Tina Holland, Fr. Michael Sullivan, Robert Kloska, Chuck Ball, Louis Albarran, Dianne Barlas, David Lutz, and Andrew Polaniecki.

I also benefited greatly from the editing of Molly Gettinger, whose love for grammar will be shared with all who read this book. Br. Nich Perez provided the graphic used in the Introduction to describe my project. The students in my Theology of Reconciliation class also provided tremendous insight to improve this book. I also am grateful to Annie McGowan, who helped work through one of the rare texts of Aquinas not yet available in English—she working from the French while I toiled with the Latin.

My application of penitential themes to the three case studies benefited from illuminating conversations over the years with Bomani Ben-Yisrayl and Peter Gehred (criminal justice); Guliver Rojas, Fr. Gustavo Gutiérrez, and Fr. David Farrell (truth and reconciliation in Peru); and Joshua Casteel, Tom Cornell, and Shawn Storer (returning soldiers). In addition, this book is permeated with insights gleaned from many years of friendship with Michael Baxter, who taught me how to think theo-politically.

I would like to acknowledge most of all my wife, Catherine, for her love and support throughout this project, which at times had a distinctly penitential impact on her. And through it all, Catherine, you are still shining like the sun! To our two young sons, Benedict and Basil: I hope that by the time you read this you have become experts in brotherly reconciliation. I also thank my in-laws, Gregory and Patricia (Mamita) Gehred, who, along with my mother, Peggy Griffin, have been a tremendous source of encouragement and joy. *Deo gratias!*

1

Introducing the Politics of Penance

"Bless me Father, for I have sinned," says the penitent to open the dialogue in Catholic confessionals across the globe and throughout the ages. After the disclosure of sins and just before the bestowal of absolution comes the priest's response, "For your penance, . . ." These lines have become iconic, providing a window into a unique element of Catholic life. But does this script, and the practices it signifies, have any relevance beyond the confessional? More specifically, does the structured imposition of a penance in the context of reconciliation work only in a church setting, or does it point to ways in which political communities can deal with acts of injustice? Exploring this question does not imply that the practice of penance within the church always works well. Too often the practice has become spiritualized—"For your penance, say three Hail Marys"—without tending also to making amends concretely. And for many Catholics, even the word *penance* suggests a sense of guilt-inducing confessionals and the root cause of a mass exodus from the sacrament. But, while I am interested in how penance can re-emerge in a contemporary revival of Confession, my focus in this book is different. I want to examine the nature of penitential action itself and explore what role it can play in solutions to social challenges ranging from crime and punishment to war and reconciliation.

The specific question I seek to answer is this: can political tasks of social repair benefit from insights on the nature of penance? An affirmative answer to this question is by no means obvious. Ethics that emphasize penance are not the first place political leaders turn in seeking tools after the rupture of communal life. Institutions like courts and prisons are the primary delegates in the pursuit of justice and reparation—if reparation is even an agreed-upon goal. A topic like penance seems, at best, a nonthreatening sideshow to this official work, perhaps complementary but certainly not a constitutive part of the justice being sought. In this way, the centrality of penance to the political tasks of social repair is not currently clear. And I am well aware that the Christian tradition itself offers not a single but multiple, and often competing, understandings of penance. My task is to mine this broad tradition in the construction of a single coherent concept of penance that can then be applied to public tasks of social repair. If I succeed, the result will be what I call a *penitential ethic*. By making this my constructive proposal, I will not be attempting to migrate this or that historical model of ecclesial practice into politics. Rather, I will glean key principles of the penitential tradition that can appeal even to a secular construal of justice, and then I will suggest how they fill gaps in the practices of social reparation today.

To begin, I offer my first and most important definition. By *penance*, I mean practices through which persons lament, take responsibility for, and seek to repair the wounds that are caused by sin. I will continue to develop this and other definitions throughout the book, but given the centrality of penance to my project, I will now highlight the three key elements of its practice:

> *Lament*, by which victims and/or perpetrators express the pain and sorrow resulting from the moral and material harm done. The community also displays a capacity for lament when it engages in self-critical dialogue and encourages individuals and institutions to consider ways we contribute to injustice.

> *Responsibility*, which includes punishment and other measures of moral accountability for wrongdoing. Penance, in fact, has been construed in Christian tradition as a kind of restorative punishment for sin. While many see reconciliation and punishment as rivals, I see them as complementary—if rightly understood.

> *Reparation*, which seeks both restitution and, when possible, the more expansive goal of restoring right relationship in the wake of injustice. Key here will be the concept, drawn from Christian tradition, of satisfaction: working to make whole what has been broken. Satisfaction is seen climactically in the work of Jesus Christ.

In important ways these three practices are sequential. That is, they establish the ideal movements by which penance becomes social repair. However, I do not want to over-script the process, and I will need to develop the interrelated dynamics of these elements. I also will need to address how insights from *theologically laden* practices and principles of penance can help meet challenges that arise, ostensibly, from *political* contexts. In this way, my use of the term *ethic* is designed for easier migration from theology to politics, but I still need to justify its relevance for pluralistic settings. I will do so by digging to the natural roots of penitential practices in order to unearth basic strategies for the social repair of human communities. The three main principles guiding these strategies are the following:

> *Individual moral agency*, which preserves personal responsibility in the wake of wrongdoing and involves its direct actors in the work of repair. This principle is at the heart of restitution and establishes for perpetrators a set of expectations tied closely to the needs of victims.

> *Communal solidarity*, which widens the scope of who participates in lamenting, taking responsibility for, and seeking to repair social wounds. Solidarity does not substitute for individual action but rather establishes a culture of participation in which multiple layers of reparation can be developed.

> *A horizon of hope*, which generates fresh motivation to construct a new social reality. Without this hope, reparation is a backward-looking and dreary burden. Yet when construed and constructed in the context of hope, social repair offers to those involved in wrongdoing the possibility of being inscribed into a new world.

As I develop the practices and principles of penance, I will use concrete examples to show their relevance and capacity to promote social repair. Specifically, I will apply the penitential ethic to the following three cases:

> *Criminal Justice*, specifically the ongoing dilemma of mass incarceration in the United States. This crisis has transformed penitentiaries into ineffective models of rehabilitation and centers of institutionalized violence that are stretching the budgetary and moral limits of society.

> *Truth and Reconciliation*, specifically in the wake of political violence. I will focus on Peru, where the failure of reparations for victims has left society fractured. Yet these conclusions are relevant in many post-conflict settings where those with political power refuse to lament, take responsibility for, and repair wounds.

> *The Return from War*, specifically the crisis of U.S. soldiers returning from Iraq and Afghanistan. These veterans have a frightening suicide rate, which is contrasted by much functional indifference

in the rest of society. While focus is given to treatment for PTSD, many soldiers are also suggesting a moral, even penitential, dimension to their recovery.

Connecting the practices and principles of penance to these cases yields the following schematic to conceptualize my project:

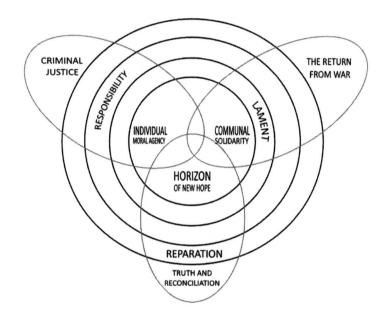

While the case for the penitential ethic will rise or fall with the power of these concepts to respond to political challenges, the most captivating dimension of the project comes through the illustrative embodiment of penance by my main sources. Thus I offer a chapter to each of these exemplars. I begin with the Irish monks of the fifth through ninth centuries, who developed a robust system of penances that were interpersonal, involving perpetrators in the process of seeing and undoing the damage of their sins. Making use of indigenous Celtic tradition as well as early Christian theology, the monasteries of Ireland became sites of reconciliation that injected socially reparative penance into violence-riven communities.

After a brief treatment of penitential theology after the monks, I turn to St. Thomas Aquinas. In the thirteenth century, Aquinas challenged conventional wisdom and insisted on a critical difference between restitution and penance. The latter, which he saw as perfecting the former, enables the penitent to participate in the graced performance of Christ's redemption of the world. This approach is connected to the aforementioned horizon of hope, in which penance can be a gift that does not so much return communities to a prior situation as it does generate creative directions by which they can build something new.

Following another treatment of historical context, we meet Pope John Paul II, the saint who during the Jubilee Year 2000 captured global attention through public gestures of repentance for the sins of Catholics throughout history. Not without opposition, the pope's strategy yielded a cascade of efforts—secular and ecclesial—for reconciliation and justice. In describing this program of collective penance, I will note the ways it was *not* employed by American bishops in the wake of the sexual abuse crisis. This specific failure, in fact, demonstrates why the penitential ethic is a needed and promising resource for the task of social repair. And it is to this task that I turn in my final chapters, in which I apply the ethic to the three case studies, demonstrating its contemporary value.

The practical aim of this book is to show that the penitential ethic I offer is not only a model but also a tool for analysis. That is, when practitioners are constructing or evaluating a specific initiative to address damages resulting from injustice, they can ask, does it promote individual moral agency and personal responsibility? Is there a communal dimension that allows for broad participation in social repair? Does it motivate fresh movement toward a new reality and not just focus on the past? Of course, the ethic is not "one size fits all" and, in my argument, I will show why different cases elicit different elements of this tool. But I do not want to limit applicability only to the cases I discuss. Rather, I intend the penitential ethic of social repair to be supple enough to have broad implications for all sites of social repair and to be detailed enough to be specified and employed in a particular situation.

I hope that my work will show the relevance of theology and church practices for our shared political terrain. In fact, I want to show that there is a kind of politics inherent in the practice of penance. By making explicit that politics and mining it—preserving what I see as the best elements of it—I will offer an ethic that is both theologically rooted and politically potent for societies in need of repair. I want to be clear, however, that lessons from the politics of penance are not just another means by which the church can teach and correct society. Rather, these lessons can also be applied *ad intra*. Church practices themselves, including the sacrament, need to be strengthened in their relational, creative, and communal dimensions in order to avoid the omnipresent dilemma of "cheap reconciliation," whereby the mercy of God is detached from justice and its challenging call to reparation. Nonetheless, the main focus of my argument will be the relevance of an ethic rooted in Christian tradition for the larger task—shared by religious and secular people alike—of social repair.

Penance in Christian Tradition

The call to reconciliation is a good description for what the early Christians saw as the very nature of God's activity in the world. The Gospels are replete with references to the reconciling work of Jesus. Healing miracles brought social inclusion; exhortations brought reminders to forgive seventy-seven times (Matt 18:22); followers were to leave gifts at the altar and go to be reconciled (Matt 5:24). Jesus gives to Peter and then to the community— "wherever two or three are gathered in my name"—the power to bind and loose sins (Matt 16:19; 18:18, 20). This same power appears in John's Gospel when the risen Jesus offers the disciples peace, bestows the Holy Spirit, and tells them, "Whose sins you forgive are forgiven them, and whose sins you retain are retained" (John 20:23). For the earliest followers of Jesus, the church clearly had been given power over sin and a mission to be "ambassadors for Christ," who has "given us the ministry of reconciliation" (2 Cor 5:18–20). What, then, is the key tool of this ministry of reconciliation? In the remainder of this chapter, I argue that it is *penance*, and I defend a particular conceptualization of it that is faithful to Christian tradition but also applicable to the wider arena of politics.

The public ministry of Jesus begins with his words, "This is the time of fulfillment. The kingdom of God is at hand. Repent, and believe in the Gospel" (Mark 1:15). This sense of repentance is not simply feeling bad about some unfortunate circumstance; it is a painful acknowledgment that one is out of step and out of line with God and with others, and the time to change is now. Inculcating repentance has been key to the church's reconciling practices. Consider this claim of Alexander Schmemann:

> It is when [we are] challenged with the real "contents" of the Gospel, with its Divine depth and wisdom, beauty and all embracing meaning, that [we] become "capable of repentance," for true

repentance is precisely the discovery of the abyss that separates [us] from God.[1]

Put another way, the first step toward life in the kingdom of God is the recognition that we are not yet there. Acts of penance, while directed toward the constructive goal of right relationship with God and repair of the social order, also work on the underlying "abyss" that causes sin in the first place.

In order to be constructive, penance must avoid two extremes. If construed as a constant reminder of one's sinful state, penance can fuel self-hatred and become destructive. But if we become too enchanted with the meritorious credit penance can accumulate, it can be reduced to one more contemporary form of self-congratulation. In light of these dangers, the word that perhaps best describes the authentic journey of penance is *conversion*, which Mark Searle called the "purpose of all ritual."[2] And conversion, I would argue, is the best way to understand the two major forms of penance that have emerged in Christian tradition: the sacrament of penance and penitential actions. While I will delve into historical instantiations of these forms in subsequent chapters, it is appropriate to present their basic shape in current Catholic theology and practice in order to gain a sense of how and why penance is an important tool that the Christian tradition has to offer—promoting social repair through personal conversion.

The *Catechism of the Catholic Church* begins its treatment of "the Sacrament of Penance and Reconciliation" by describing it as "the sacrament of conversion."[3] Contemporary Catholics, of course, associate the sacrament mainly with the element of confession, and yet, in traditional terms, this element is bookended by two others: contrition and satisfaction, the latter of which refers to the process by which we participate in the healing justice offered by Christ, who alone satisfactorily responds to sin. It is within this final element of satisfaction that the formal role of a penance emerges. The work of penance thus involves divine and human agency, with interior and exterior ramifications. Consider the way the *Catechism* understands the function of a penance: "One must do what is possible in order to repair the harm (e.g., return stolen goods, restore the reputation of someone slandered, pay compensation for injuries). Simple justice requires as much."[4] But this alone is not satisfaction. The penitent must do "something more

---

1. Schmemann, "Some Reflections on Confession," 41.
2. Searle, "Journey of Conversion," 47.
3. *Catechism of the Catholic Church*, 1423.
4. Ibid., 1459.

to make amends" and thus "make satisfaction" for sins by seeking healing at the level of "relationships" with God and others.[5] Personal conversion is thus tied to social repair.

To be sure, the reparative nature of penance is not always emphasized in the popular experience of the sacrament. On this point, Nathan Mitchell has referenced the well-known critique, offered by Godfrey Diekmann, aimed at those for whom confession is practiced as a kind of "private soul therapy," which "almost seems to be a cop out in the face of pressing social concerns for reconciliation. It claims to provide one with a 'clean slate,' even when we know that, socially, nobody's slate is clean . . . Instead of taking away guilt it takes away the sense of social responsibility and dulls the truly human conscience."[6]

Insights of this kind have led to vigorous debate in the church over the reform of the sacrament. One suggestion has been that absolution should *conclude* a process of penance, the word of forgiveness thus ratifying the reparation that has been accomplished. Indeed, as we will see, in the early church, this model prevailed. On the other hand, such a model can risk seeing forgiveness as earned. And the placement of absolution before penance affirms the gospel sense that forgiveness is to be celebrated as a gratuitous gift and an invitation to extend the repairing power of Christ into the world. In either case, Diekmann's insight does highlight the danger of dropping a robust sense of the penitent's work—or, rather, the work they share with God—from sacramental practice. As the *Catechism*, echoing the Council of Trent, makes clear, "Absolution takes away sin, but it does not remedy all the disorders sin has caused."[7] Penance is designed for just this task, and thus, while the practice of the sacrament today does not always illustrate it, the church's own self-understanding emphasizes that penance has a highly reparative nature.

Penance as a Social Practice

While most people associate the concept of penance with the sacrament, penitential practices actually have a much broader role in Christian social ethics. It is thus helpful to highlight now the more expansive notion, since the larger project of this book requires the ability to migrate the logic of

5. Ibid.

6. Mitchell, *Rite of Penance*, 86.

7. *Catechism*, 1459.

penance into arenas outside the church. Turning again to the *Catechism*, we see this move already anticipated, with a section titled "The Many Forms of Penance in Christian Life." The treatment begins with the traditional ecclesial practices of fasting, prayer, and almsgiving. Key themes, already noted as rooted in a reparative concept of penance, are invoked to describe these traditional practices as ones "which express conversion in relation to oneself, to God, and to others."[8] The forms of penance that "are means of obtaining forgiveness of sins" then grow to include "efforts at reconciliation with one's neighbor, tears of repentance, concern for the salvation of one's neighbor, the intercession of the saints, and the practice of charity, 'which covers a multitude of sins.'"[9] To emphasize the expansive nature of practices in which "conversion is accomplished in daily life," the *Catechism* also then notes "gestures of reconciliation, concern for the poor, the exercise and defense of justice and right, the admission of one's faults to one's brethren, fraternal correction, revision of life, examination of conscience, spiritual direction, acceptance of suffering, endurance of persecution for the sake of righteousness."[10]

The list of forms of penance is not meant to be an exhaustive catalog of penitential options. Rather, it illustrates that the church's understanding of the concept includes a vast array of reparative social practices and little of the stereotypical sense of penance as an exercise in self-loathing guilt. This is important, because to suggest that penances are practices of love that repair the social order will strike some as revisionist, as if this concept were designed to elude the critique of moderns. Yet the list just invoked resonates with the notion of penance in biblical tradition and is also remarkably similar to the approach developed in the early church, as we will see. Penance in the Christian tradition is thus a *constellation* of practices, each of which resonates with the goal of persons lamenting, taking responsibility for, and seeking to repair the wounds that are caused by sin. Moreover, penance is done not only in response to *one's own sins*; it also capacitates persons to repair the harms of injustices for which they are not directly responsible. In this sense, penance is a communal practice that may be used to confront the reality of a world that is not as it should be. This is a deeply social logic that responds well, I will argue, to many complex injustices that beset contemporary society. In other words, the social nature of penance

8. Ibid., 1434.
9. Ibid.
10. Ibid., 1435.

corresponds to the social nature of sin, which often makes it difficult to ascertain clear and simple lines of culpability.

The paradigmatic example of communal penance in the Christian tradition is Lent. Perhaps one anecdotal way to confirm the importance of penance in human life is to note the attendance, always higher than usual, at Ash Wednesday services. I will not rehearse here the history of Lent, but its emergence and current prominence—now adopted increasingly in the Protestant world, too—make an important point that connects penance to the church's understanding of the repairing power bequeathed to it by Christ. Originally a time to prepare catechumenates for baptism at Easter, Lent became used also as the time to prepare public sinners to re-experience the power of their own baptism in the Easter liturgies. As awareness of the universal need for conversion grew, the emergence of Lent inscribed *all Christians* into the penitential community seeking reconciliation. Thus, Lent has functioned as the primary means for the development of a theology and practice of penance that is communal in nature.

Today, some see Lent as a time to adopt various forms of privation and suffering, yet suffering for its own sake would elude the definition of penance that I have put forward. Rather, the traditional practices of Lent—prayer, fasting, and almsgiving—present an interesting mix of opportunities for personal conversion and social repair, touching on all three dimensions I put forward—lament, responsibility, and repair. Consider also how the season of Lent has become a key time of growth for social justice ministries in the church. Operation Rice Bowl, the longtime Lenten campaign that provides significant funding for Catholic Relief Services through the filling of small donation boxes, is evidence of the traditional link between penitential practice and social repair. While Lent is sometimes still experienced as a gloomy time of self-loathing, this again is not the church's understanding. In fact, we can even say that Lent can be *celebrated*: the preface used in the Eucharistic Prayer during Lent offers thanks to God for "this joyful season."

Through sacrament and in daily life, then, the church puts forward numerous practices of penance as part of the "ministry of reconciliation" by which we share the reconciling power bestowed on us by Christ. As the list noted above shows, these practices—fraternal correction, works of mercy, and the defense of justice, to name a few—all have a specifically penitential dimension. In doing them, we *lament* the reality of sin and injustice and actively seek to restore right relationship. These practices also illustrate the extent to which penance is the domain of all Christians, creating a strong role for the laity in deploying the church's reconciling resources. John Paul II made this call explicit in saying during his World Day of Peace Message in 1997 that "in a certain sense, every baptized person must consider himself a 'minister of reconciliation.'"[11]

What we might describe as "the universal call to penitence"—applicable to all, even when not in response to the direct commission of serious sin—should not detract from another function of penance after situations of very direct, and very serious, sin. That function involves penance as the safeguard against the aforementioned concept of "cheap reconciliation." This phrase is rooted in Dietrich Bonhoeffer's classic maxim about grace in *The Cost of Discipleship*: "Cheap grace is the grace we bestow on ourselves. Cheap grace is the preaching of forgiveness without requiring repentance."[12] In the arena of reconciliation, Bonhoeffer saw this danger as amounting to "the justification of sin without the justification of the repentant sinner who departs from sin and from whom sin departs."[13] Such a paradigm is also why Bonhoeffer lamented the disappearance of most forms of confession in the Protestant tradition, since it meant the loss of a space in which "there takes place a breakthrough to community."[14] Again, this does not mean that cheap grace is never on offer in Catholic confessionals, but it displays the reason why acts of penance are a particularly important element in the church's ministry of reconciliation. Especially in light of serious sins that tear at the fabric of community, attention to penance keeps in view the victims' need for restitution, society's need for restoration, and the offender's need for reformation. Again, this social logic will be explored in further chapters.

Penance thus guards against cheap reconciliation, calling us to put "skin in the game," but I want to repeat here that this should not diminish reconciliation as God's gratuitous gift. To be sure, the fear of "earned forgiveness" has historically made many non-Catholics uneasy with a strong emphasis on penance. Jesus, it is asserted, freely forgave. In the paradigmatic parable, while the lost son "was still a long way off," the prodigal father, "filled with compassion," "ran to his son" and welcomed him home to "celebrate with a feast" (Luke 15:20–23). Here we see the gratuitous gift of

11. John Paul II, "Offer Forgiveness and Receive Peace," 457.

12. Bonhoeffer, *Cost of Discipleship*, 44.

13. Ibid.

14. Bonhoeffer, *Life Together*, 110.

reconciliation on display without, so it seems, the corresponding element of penance. And yet, even in this challenging test case for the penitential tradition, we can find surprising resources. First, the son's experience in the distant country, where he is close to "dying of hunger," turns out to be a form of penance, undesired for sure, but a consequence of his sin and a spur toward reformation—a sign that penances work on the physical as well as spiritual level. Second, in the plan for his confession, the son does in fact intend to make a promise of penance: "treat me as you would treat one of your hired workers" (Luke 15:19). It may be the case that this is less than sincere (though the text does not make this assumption) and it is also true that the father stops him right before he is able to articulate his intention. Still, we do not know that the father does *not* intend to implement a program of reparation *after* the celebration. In fact, seeing the two as compatible—a gratuitous offer of forgiveness and the hard work of restoration—resonates with the larger narrative of the Gospels, in which Jesus' actions of healing and forgiveness initiate a move toward a new way of life.

To summarize, I have briefly sketched a theological definition of penance as the practices through which persons lament, take responsibility for, and seek to repair the wounds that are caused by sin. This definition squares with Christian tradition and with contemporary Catholic teaching, though I acknowledge that, in practice, this theology is in need of better performance. Moreover, I have argued that the best way to understand penance is as a tool at the service of reparation within the church's ministry of reconciliation. In this ministry, to which all the baptized are called in one way or another, we share the healing power of the risen Christ. We also, I will now argue, participate in a logic and a politics that can be employed outside the church, and even in the most public of arenas.

Penance and Politics

One of the great historians of penance, Paul Galtier, analyzed a broad survey of pre-Christian and non-Christian religions from diverse parts of the world and concluded that "penance is of natural origin . . . [It is] the first sign of the moral sense."[15] He cites evidence from Confucianism, Hinduism, and Buddhism, among others, to show that in other traditions there exist paradigms of "confession and expiation of faults."[16] It would be beyond

15. Galtier, *Origines du Sacrément de Pénitence*, in Riga, *Sin and Penance*, 66.
16. Ibid.

the scope of this book to examine the many and varied forms penance has taken in the vast religious history of human beings. Moreover, as I have noted, I am more interested in developing a particular ethic of penance that is rooted in Christian practice and that reflects not just religious culture but human nature as such. One contemporary political theorist who sees great promise in mining religious tradition in this way is Daniel Philpott. While many moderns are reluctant to see religious tradition as a source of political wisdom, Philpott does not draw such thick boundary lines. He suggests that by taking religious sources seriously—using Judaism, Christianity, and Islam as his primary examples—modern practicioners can find elements of an "overlapping consensus" on principles of social repair. And these principles, Philpott makes clear, are not unintelligible in the public square: they are examples of the "rooted reason" that emerges from religious tradition.[17] To ignore them is not to win a victory for rational discourse but to eclipse a profound resource for human reflection on the task of reconciliation.

Thomas Aquinas agrees. Aquinas, who saw penance not only as a practice but as a virtue, did not think virtue was the domain of Christians alone. Aquinas argued that the rational inclination toward penance, as toward all natural virtue, is a universal human phenomenon: "It is a natural law that one should repent of the evil one has done, by grieving for having done it and by seeking a remedy."[18] To be sure, Aquinas does clarify that in the sacramental encounter this natural inclination is deepened by the infusion of grace. But, as I will show at length in chapter 3, grace does not eclipse the rational, natural element, and penance remains for Aquinas a virtue of justice. More to the present point, Aquinas' sense of penance here confirms my own definition of penance as practices through which persons lament, take responsibility for, and seek to repair the wounds that are caused by sin. Interestingly, he emphasizes its natural context through the story of Jonah's mission to Nineveh, home to a pagan people at odds with Israel. As Aquinas notes, in the biblical narrative penance was *their* idea, not Jonah's: "They proclaimed a fast and all of them, great and small, put on sackcloth" (Jonah 3:5). Their penance caused a quite surprising result: "When God saw by their actions how they turned from their evil way, he repented of the evil that he had threatened to do to them. He did not carry it out" (Jonah 3:10). Aquinas is clear that the penance of the pagan Ninevites is as yet imperfect, but it shows the wide natural scope of the practice and

---

17. Philpott, *Just and Unjust Peace*, 112.

18. Aquinas, *Summa theologiae*, III.84.a7, ad1.

illustrates his principle that grace perfects nature. In fact, the success of the Ninevites might even suggest that nature was perfecting grace! Of course, *both* nature and grace are aspects of divine providence, but my point here is simply to note Aquinas' emphasis on the rationality and universality of the practice of penance.

Indeed, the relationship between the natural scope of penance in human experience and its particular performance in Christian tradition is the key to the project of this book. For Christians who believe that the world is created in Christ, it should come as no surprise that his reparative power moves, ultimately, with the grain of the universe.[19] But this does not mean, of course, that Christian practices can simply be "migrated" into the political order or "translated" into political axioms. And, thus, it is important at this point for me to pause and briefly offer the theology of political engagement that drives my project. That is, how do I construe the task of bringing theological insight to bear on politics? And what is the role of the church, of the state, and of the many other actors—both individuals and institutions—who are relevant to the work of social repair?

At the Second Vatican Council, major questions about the implication of Christian practice for the pursuit of justice in politics were addressed in *Gaudium et spes*, the Pastoral Constitution on the Church in the Modern World. There, the Council begins its treatment of "What the Church Offers to Society" with a note of caution: "Christ did not bequeath to the Church a mission in the political, economic or social order: the purpose he assigned to it was a religious one."[20] In more recent times, Pope Benedict XVI affirmed this perspective by arguing that the church "cannot and must not replace the State," since "a just society must be the achievement of politics, not of the Church."[21] While this emphasis on the distinction between the ecclesial and civil spheres might seem to suggest that political questions are of secondary importance to Catholics, in fact, the point at work here is to emphasize the distinctive contribution we can make in that realm. As the Council puts it, "The impact which the Church can have on modern society amounts to an effective living of faith and love, not to any external power exercised by purely human means."[22] This construal of the church's role

19. The phrase here is an axiom for the work of John Howard Yoder in his attempt to advance a doctrine of creation that shows both Christian distinctiveness and universal relevance. See also Hauerwas, *With the Grain of the Universe*.

20. *Gaudium et spes*, 42.

21. Pope Benedict XVI, *Deus caritas est*, 28.

22. *Gaudium et spes*, 42.

does not minimize the political implications of the gospel—such a move would suggest a limit to Christ's repairing power in the world—but rather specifies three ways in which Christian practice is to be shared. First, the role of the laity comes into sharp focus. Second, the rational dimension of ecclesial practice is highlighted. And third, the way in which practices stoke political imagination reveals their relevance for the civic arena. These three points constitute the basic elements in the theology of political engagement that will drive my project. Each point will be explicated throughout the book, but I will offer a brief summary here.

If Christianity is to transform political structures for the better, it will come not from the wielding of institutional power but from the work and witness of Christians in all walks of civic life. Indeed, in *Christifidelis laici*, a manifesto on the greatness of the lay vocation, John Paul II makes precisely this point by invoking key sentiments from *Gaudium et spes*:

> The lay faithful, in fact, "are called by God so that they, led by the spirit of the Gospel, might contribute to the sanctification of the world, as from within like leaven, by fulfilling their own particular duties. Thus, especially in this way of life, resplendent in faith, hope and charity they manifest Christ to others." Thus for the lay faithful, to be present and active in the world is not only an anthropological and sociological reality, but in a specific way, a theological and ecclesiological reality as well. In fact, in their situation in the world God manifests his plan and communicates to them their particular vocation of "seeking the Kingdom of God by engaging in temporal affairs and by ordering them according to the plan of God."[23]

Here we see the primary way in which I envision the ethic of reparation I propose being brought to the political arena. Like members of all traditions, Christians occupy places in the many and varied political institutions of the world. In these arenas, which often have a direct role in tasks of social repair, public officials would be derelict not to make use of approaches and principles that can aid their political task of promoting the justice of healthy relationships and the common good. An official who is also Catholic might regard a given political situation as a potential site of "sanctification," but this should deepen their commitment to the common good rather than excuse them from acting in a way that fits it.

---

23. Pope John Paul II, *Christifidelis laici*, 15.

The second element of my theology of political engagement highlights the continuity of faith and reason. As noted, I work from the proposition that the power of Christ to repair the world is in no competition with our rational capacity to develop logical responses to social problems. Moreover, the very structure of penitential work in the church's mission of reconciliation is rooted in a universal human phenomenon of regret and repair—principles Galtier ascribes to "natural origin" and Aquinas to "natural law." Thus, my proposal of an ethic of social repair is based on the need for rational responses to problems that face the human community and not just Christians alone. The more rational and effective, I believe, the more consistent the ethic will be with the way God made us, prone to discord but ordered to reconciliation. Following Philpott's concept of "rooted reason," rationality becomes a welcome test for the ethic I propose. This is not an additional obstacle to public justification imposed only on theological ethics—in the manner of John Rawls, who sees religious approaches in some tension with reason.[24] Rather, the ability of any ethic—religious or not—to provide a compelling public rationale gets to the heart of what Philpott calls the empirical "legitimacy" of the ethic: "The wider the set of people who endorse it and the more deeply they hold the belief, the more likely it is to succeed."[25] In this way, the foundation of the ethic I propose is its capacity to respond rationally and effectively to the actual needs of diverse human communities seeking social repair.

In distinction to those who tend to single out religious ethics as particularly marginal to politics, I will argue that theological ethics are especially relevant to the civic arena. The reason—which is the third element in my approach to political engagement—is their capacity to stoke the social imagination. John De Gruchy argues that "the problem with the widespread secular world-view is the inability to imagine alternatives."[26] In this sense, the best opening argument for the relevance of the penitential tradition to political life today is the obvious need for new approaches to reconciliation—be it in the wake of violent crime, war, or any other destructive social force. Historically, many of our secular, public institutions do have their roots in religious practice. Consider, for example, the modern penitentiary. The word *penitentiary* itself can remind us of the seemingly forgotten fact that this institution carries a connection to penitential tradition. This is just

24. See Philpott, *Just and Unjust Peace*, 106.

25. Ibid., 116.

26. De Gruchy, *Reconciliation*, 211.

one example of the many ways in which religious tradition is not wholly "other" to secular politics. Religious people, after all, have faced all the same challenges to human community that everyone has. We have our blind spots, to be sure, but so do secular perspectives, and a mutual dialogue can be illuminative for all. Thus, as a Catholic steeped in my own tradition and as a fellow citizen of the world, I will engage the challenge of reconciliation facing the human community by offering a penitential ethic. And I will do so with the hope of stoking our collective political imagination.

The theological root sustaining each of the above elements of my practical approach to political engagement is summed up well by N. T. Wright, who takes up the question usually posed to an ethic such as mine: "Why should Christian morality be good for non-Christians?" The answer emerges through

> the claim that in Jesus of Nazareth the creator of the world—the whole world, not a Christian subset of the world!—is being rescued and renewed. Of course, non-Christians will say they don't believe this. But Christians do, or at least should—and are therefore committed to believing that the new creation launched in Jesus is good news for *all* people at *every* level, so that even if people do not share explicit Christian faith it will still be a better, wiser, and fairer world if people live with the grain of the universe, which we see in Jesus and in the way of life he modeled and articulated.[27]

To this strong theology of creation, through which God, the Father of all, shapes every human person in and toward the image of God the Son, I would add emphasis on the action of God the Holy Spirit. The movement of the Spirit "with the grain of the universe" allows a bridge between practices of the *ecclesia* and of the *polis*. Aquinas himself proposes the principle "Deus non alligatur sacramentis," God is not bound by the sacraments.[28] That is, while the church provides the most stable and lasting means of grace in the world, divine providence is on display elsewhere, too. Thus only with a strong sense of a lively Holy Spirit at work in the whole world can I maintain a strong emphasis on *both* the universal relevance of a penitential ethic *and* its clear embodiment in the church.

In this context, I can conclude this brief sketch of my theology of political engagement with a caution from De Gruchy. He warns of a "danger of speaking about reconciliation," namely that we move too quickly from

---

27. Wright, *Scripture and the Authority of God,* 192–93.

28. Aquinas, *Summa theologiae,* III 68.2

religious concepts to political application. He proposes rather a "primary" and "secondary" meaning of reconciliation. The primary level of meaning, on display in the life of the church, is distinct from secondary expressions, which are "visible in social and political reality even though, for the Christian, they have their basis in that which is beyond empirical verifiability."[29] I take the primary-secondary concept as a friendly amendment. The primary meaning of penance is to facilitate the reconciliation by which the church manifests the power of the risen Christ to create a community of love. This power is not always susceptible to the calculations and measurements of public policy. Put another way, the Christian commitment to reconciliation will push toward places that our politics does not want to go, especially in its treatment of perpetrators. I am clear-eyed about that. But, as my theology of political engagement indicates, I will not pit Christian ethics against rational ethics. When robustly performed and coherently conceptualized, penitential practices can be mined for a logic that is relevant and accessible to all. And thus, while I accept the primary-secondary distinction, I will also emphasize that the political application of a theological ethic of reconciliation is not secondary *in its importance*. It is a second step, requiring ecclesial performance in order to emerge most fully, but it is no less important for the mission of the church in service to the world.

I have just sketched the elements of my theology of political engagement. In the next chapter, I will begin my attempt to demonstrate the way in which select strands of the Christian tradition of penance can aid in the challenge of imagining alternatives to currently failing systems of social repair. That mining project will take us to the Irish monasteries of the fifth to ninth centuries, to the medieval mind of Thomas Aquinas, and to the penitential witness of Pope John Paul II during the Jubilee Year 2000. To reiterate, the goal will not be to idealize an ecclesial model or suggest its transplantation to the civic arena. Rather, I will be illuminating practices and principles drawn from these resources in order to apply them to the most contemporary of political challenges facing the human community.

29. De Gruchy, *Reconciliation*, 17–18.

2

Here Come the Irish: Monks and Social Penance

WHEN HISTORIAN AND POPULAR writer Thomas Cahill proclaimed that "the Irish saved civilization," he was referencing the monks of the fifth to ninth centuries, but it was not because of their penitential practices.[1] Rather, foremost in his mind were the painstaking hours and days and years that these men and women spent transcribing and, thus, preserving the great texts of human civilization. Paradigmatic among their achievements was the great *Book of Kells*, an illustrated manuscript of the Gospels. This and other masterpieces of the monks provided rays of light during the Dark Ages—"the work, not of men, but of angels," remarked one thirteenth-century historian.[2] While the world indeed has these monks to thank for the preservation of faith and culture through their dedication to scholarship and art, less acclaimed is their contribution to the work of reconciliation. On a popular level, many give inadequate attention to the centrality that one-to-one encounters with penitents had in the life of these monks over several centuries. In theological analyses, sometimes the nature of the monks' reconciling work is described as individualistic, harsh, and rigorist. Thus, for some, even if the Irish saved civilization, their penitential practices are decidedly not part of that legacy. In this chapter, I will disagree with that analysis and, more importantly, demonstrate why the monks' practice of penance is among their most important contributions to the church and the world.

---

1 Cahill, *How the Irish Saved Civilization.*

2 See Meehan, *Book of Kells*, 9.

Many standard narratives mark a contrast between the "social" approach to penance in the early centuries of Christianity and the "individual" approach that arose in Ireland. Even the sympathetic Peter Riga, in his classic history of penance, invokes the word "private" six times in a single paragraph, contrasting the monks from earlier "public" approaches.[3] The problem with this assessment is manifold: the monasteries were ensconced in a deeply social environment, the penances prescribed were deeply social in nature, and the process was clearly aimed at social repair and restoration. The substance of these claims will be on full display in this chapter, but I need to foreground them in order to emphasize the way that the monks not only did not depart from but actually built on the social practices of the early church, particularly the Order of Penitents. No doubt, the Irish penitentials sprung from other seeds as well—the monastic tradition, Eastern spirituality, and local custom, each of which will be examined in turn—but first it is necessary to situate the monks in the context of the Western ecclesial tradition that had prevailed before them.

The Order of Penitents

James Dallen, in his theological history, *The Reconciling Community*, notes that we cannot speak of a single system of penance that dominated the early church. By region and by time period, practices varied widely. Two main early trajectories, however, can be noted as "rigorist" and "pastoralist." For both, serious sin in the church was no light matter. In becoming a member of this minority community, Dallen notes, "individuals left their former selves behind and bound themselves by the baptismal *sacramentum* to live by the Spirit of Jesus."[4] Of course, disputes and infractions would occur, and, then as now, many practices brought reconciliation—charity, fraternity, and Eucharist prominent among them. But what about grave sins, like the triad listed in Acts 15:29—adultery, apostasy, and murder? Even here, Dallen notes, early letters from Clement (around the year 96) and the text of the *Didache* (early 100s) do not prescribe a separate ritual for these sins but, rather, urge prudential separation, correction, and reconciliation before returning to the Eucharist so that, as the *Didache* puts it, "your sacrifice may be pure."[5] Yet it is clear that, over time, some leaders feared that lax

3. Riga, *Sin and Penance*, 104.

4. Dallen, *Reconciling Community*, 18.

5. Ibid., 19–21.

Christians (church membership was growing, and many had been baptized as infants) were taking advantage of the presumption for reconciliation and, thus, making post-baptismal sin less exceptional and more tolerable.

The presence of those who argued that baptism provided the only "plank of repentance" is attested to by a text written in the early to mid-100s, known as *The Shepherd of Hermas*, which argues for a more pastoral view. Since the church, where "God's pardon is present and active," is still "under construction," even serious sinners—and even after baptism—have "a last chance for repentance."[6] This represented a *paenitentia secunda*, second penance (the first being offered in the journey to baptism). Hermas did not envision multiple opportunities for this, mainly because he expected the final judgment of God to be close at hand. But the church increasingly accepted his position that with repentance, acts of charity, and the prayers of church elders, the sinner can be joyfully re-received once. Chief among the rivals to this view was Tertullian, a Christian convert writing in the early 200s, who inveighed against "the shepherd of adulterers," arguing that there were post-baptismal sins that the church simply could *never* forgive.[7] Interestingly, Tertullian originally did allow for the single, exceptional possibility of post-baptismal penance for serious sinners. His process involved a kind of "penitential institution" in which sinners would be kept as a distinct group and subject to a rigorous program of discipline, since "the Church must test sincerity through external manifestations."[8] The subjugation—embodied in acts such as kneeling in sackcloth and ashes at the church entrance each Sunday—would be lifted with eucharistic re-entry and what Tertullian called "reincorporation into the Church."[9] While Tertullian ultimately broke with the Catholic practice of re-reception, his model attests to the growth of an *ordo paenitentium*, order of penitents, in the early church.

In his book *The Order of Penitents*, Joseph Favazza notes the multivalent nature of the term *ordo*. In the first place, it referred to a group of persons within the church. Such a group could be permanent, like the *ordo sacerdotum* of priests, or transitional, like the *ordo catechumenorum* of those preparing for baptism.[10] It was as a transitional group that the order

6. Ibid., 22.

7. Ibid., 23.

8. Ibid., 31–32.

9. Ibid., 34.

10. Favazza, *Order of Penitents*, 235–37. For the term *ordo penitentium*, see ibid., 61.

of penitents emerged in the first three centuries of Christianity. A second meaning of *ordo*, as "structured process," is also relevant here. Not that there was uniformity in how local churches dealt with serious post-baptismal sin, but a basic process can be identified. First, it involved exclusion, during which the penitent still had status within the church but was relegated to some form of separation in the gathered community, such as departing from the liturgy before the consecration and reception of the Eucharist. Second, it involved *exomologesis*, confession. This term can be misleading, since some take it to mean that penitents were required to confess their sins aloud before the community. Such a public confession was mentioned, for example, by Irenaeus in the mid-100s. The purpose here was not so much to disclose a specific sin, but rather to repent publicly for what the tight-knit community likely already knew.[11] In general, exomologesis referred to the sinner's—and the whole church's—confession of faith in Christ's forgiving mercy and did *not* usually involve naming aloud one's sins. The third element of the *ordo* was penance. During this period, the penitents would be exhorted to spend time in prayer, to practice fasting, and to be generous in works of mercy.[12] Finally, there was re-entry and welcome from the community, often during the Holy Thursday liturgy and often with a "laying on of hands" by the bishop.

Thus, the church's earliest practices treated sin, penance, and reconciliation in light of the serious and public consequences of baptism, and this approach emerged in a structured way with the formation of an order of penitents. Still, how this process unfolded continued to vary greatly from place to place and time to time. For example, Favazza notes that while the "unrepeatability of ecclesial penance as an accepted disciplinary norm of the Church" prevailed in the West, in the East multiple reconciliations were common.[13] And, even in the West, the proponents of unrepeatability emerge most strongly after Constantine began the shift to Christianity as the state religion. And thus it was, argues Favazza, "in an effort to brace up the ancient penitential discipline in the face of mass conversions" that the unrepeatability of penance becomes cemented as the norm.[14] At this time, too, heightened concern to resist the laxity that came with larger

11. Ibid., 110.

12. While these works were clearly seen as restorative, it is not clear that they were designed to involve restitution as such. This is an area for further research.

13. Ibid., 248–49.

14. Ibid., 249.

numbers of Christians led to more systematized control over the remission of sins. The system that developed is properly called, according to Favazza, *canonical penance*, which carries forward some elements of the order of penitents but with critical changes. Most notable among them was that canonical penance often brought "juridical restraints" that were imposed for life, even after the one-time readmission to the community. For example, reconciled sinners often were banned from holding ecclesial or public office.[15] For these reasons, Favazza distinguishes the earlier order of penitents from the emergence of canonical penance, and he suggests that a medicinal approach to penance gave way to a more punitive view by which sinners were marked for life as second-class members of the church.[16]

Not surprisingly, a popular response to the many restraints of canonical penance was simply to delay it until the end of life. Two of the most prominent scholars of penance in the Christian tradition, Bernhard Poschmann and John Mahoney, concur with Favazza's analysis and highlight the major ramifications of this shift. Poschmann argues that in this post-Constantinian world, "legalistic tendencies of the Roman mind" came to the fore and created a "heavy burden to penance."[17] As a result, while canonical processes were in place, the length of the processes and the extent of the demands made ecclesial penance less relevant to the daily life of the laity. Mahoney adds that even after doing penance, "the Christian was still a marked man, disqualified for life from various activities, ranging from military service to marital relations."[18] The result, Mahoney notes, led some church leaders to protest the process. Caesarius, bishop of Arles in the sixth century, complained about canonical penance in a sermon by reading aloud the letter of one church member, who wrote, "I'm in the Army, and I'm married, how can I do penance?"[19] To be sure, catechetical texts from earlier centuries also made deep demands on catechumens as well as penitents. Interestingly, in the earlier centuries the ban on military activities was also present—though not to punish sin, but rather to prevent it, given the church's commitment to nonviolence. Nonetheless, in the post-Constantine era, the focus on penance as a practical invitation to achievable reconciliation was compromised. Poschmann concludes that the "excessive demands,

---

15. Ibid., 250.

16. Ibid., 247.

17 In Favazza, *Order of Penitents*, 251.

18. Mahoney, *Making of Moral Theology*, 4.

19. Ibid.

more than anything else, were the shoals on which the system of canonical penance would inevitably be wrecked."[20]

Here Come the Irish

As the practices of penance began their sharp decline in the Roman world, the inverse phenomenon was taking shape in Ireland. There, with monasteries blossoming among village communities, monks were increasingly being visited by penitents—fellow monks as well as local villagers—seeking reconciliation and spiritual direction toward a life free from sin. A new age was dawning. Already in the 400s, with the arrival of Patrick, the Irish were not simply receiving a migrated religion but rather one that resonated deeply with their culture. As Cahill puts it, "Patrick's gift to the Irish was his Christianity—the first de-Romanized Christianity in human history."[21] This is hyperbole on both counts: Rome did not define the entire Christian world, and Patrick was by no means detached from his Roman roots. But it does point to a truth, namely that the church in Ireland was able to develop distinct practices designed for the particular needs of its people. And nowhere was this more evident than in rituals of penance. In sharp contrast to the increasingly empty orders of penitents in the Roman world, the ranks of Irish penitents, and the monks who led them, swelled. And part of the success, as will be noted, was indeed the decidedly non-Roman practice of repeatable penance. According to Hugh Connolly, one of the leading historians of Irish penance, repeatability was informed at least in part by druidic cult practices, which strongly resisted definitive expulsions from the group.[22] This indigenous impulse, along with their fresh reading of the gospel, led the Irish to see reconciliation not as a one-time offer but as a continuous journey along the church's path.

Of course, the indigenous impulses of Ireland were not entirely toward reconciliation. The warring and bloody nature of ancient Ireland is legendary. In fact, the violence of the society into which the new Christian message broke makes the story of Irish penance all the more relevant to the violence of our own day. For example, in the ancient epic text *Táin Bó Cúailnge*, which recounts the dramas of pre-Christian Ireland, the celebration of killing is enough to rival a modern *gangsta* rapper. At one point

20. In Favazza, *Order of Penitents*, 251.

21. Cahill, *How the Irish Saved Civilization*, 148.

22. Connolly, *Irish Penitentials*, 5–6.

it praises a hero who "mowed down" his enemies, left the masses in carnage, "slew one hundred and thirty kings," and, "when the battle was over," "left without a scratch" on his chariot's "heroic frontal spikes."[23] As if the proliferation of violence in that society, as in our own, were not already a kind of human sacrifice, the ancient Irish also engaged in formal rituals of execution for the placation of bloodthirsty gods. And while Ireland did not suddenly become a halcyon utopia after the arrival of Christianity, as we will see quite clearly, historians do agree that a radical transformation of a violence-riven society was begun by missionaries like Patrick and their great numbers of new converts. Volumes have been written on the reasons for their success—and how they avoided martyrdom in achieving it—but part of their victory is explained by their novel approach to transforming vice into virtue through the practice of penance.

Before explaining in detail the kinds of penitential processes that took place in Ireland, along with the penitentials themselves—the texts that arose to guide the monks in ministering to sinners—it is necessary to examine the soil from which these practices sprung: the monastery. Indeed, the rise of the monastery as the center of Irish Catholic life provides the most important context for understanding the forms of penance that took root there. The usual triad of the early progenitors of Irish Catholicism includes bishops, like St. Patrick; hermit-ascetics, like St. Kevin; and monks, like St. Brigid and St. Finnian. But all agree that it was the monks who emerged as the key actors in the Irish church and in the historic migration of Irish monasticism—and penitential practice—to continental Europe in a kind of reverse evangelization. This reversal began with St. Columba (also known as Columcille) and his founding of the Iona monastery in Scotland.

Indeed, the story of Columba is a kind of microcosm of effective penance in the wake of violence. While Columba had massive success during the 500s—founding forty-one monasteries in forty-one years—he found trouble when he surreptitiously transcribed his teacher Finnian's prized copy of the St. Jerome Psalter. A ruling against Columba led not only to his loss of the psalter but to a bitter rivalry among locals, which ended in a war. Three thousand and one were dead, and Columba was responsible for starting it. As he faced punishment for his role, legend has it that St. Brendan intervened and suggested a program of penance: Columba would expiate his sin by an exile in which he would have to save as many souls as had been lost in the war. St. Columba embraced the penance and set sail for

23. Cahill, *How the Irish Saved Civilization*, 85–86.

the island of Iona. From the community he established there came the missionaries who spread monasticism far and wide. Interestingly, the relationship of violence, penance, and mission in Ireland may date to St. Patrick himself, who in his *Confession* refers to a great sin in his youth that many biographers conjecture was murder.[24] It was, in any case, a sin that impelled him to work with special vigor against the violent habits he encountered in the Irish people, a dedication that was embraced in the coming centuries by the monks.

The Development of Monastic Practices

This way in which the Irish monasteries were part and parcel of the social fabric of early Irish Catholic society is important in order to resist the narrative of the monks as founders of a "private" sacrament. Even Dallen adopts this standard view, describing the Irish system as "so individualized as to have lost almost all reference to the worshipping community."[25] No doubt, as we will see, the one-to-one encounter was a central feature of the Irish approach, and there was, indeed, no "order of penitents" as such, if by "order" we mean a group with a special ecclesial status. Interestingly, theologian Gerard Mitchell notes that there is some evidence that in the time of St. Patrick himself, there were in Ireland some canonical texts in use that prescribed distinctive clothing for penitents and a ritual for the laying on of hands by the bishop. Mitchell adds that St. Patrick would never have intentionally abandoned these inherited forms of canonical penance, but that the rise of the monastery as the central institution of the Irish church is what yielded the move away from canonical penance and toward the distinctively Irish approach to reconciliation.[26] In other words, it was the social and interpersonal relationships that grew out of the monastery that gave this penitential practice the force for its popularity. And contrary to Dallen's endorsement of the standard narrative here, we will see that the role of the community was quite robust, especially in response to sins that were also crimes against the social fabric.

Penitential practice emerged quite naturally from the spirituality of the monks, and thus it is important at this point to note key elements in their monastic life and how its development yielded distinctive practices

24. See ibid., 113.

25. Dallen, *Reconciling Community*, 108.

26. See Mitchell, "Origins of Irish Penance," 1–14.

of penance. Irish monks embraced what came to be called a "green martyr-dom." It was different from the "red martyrdom," which was never visited upon them (just as they did not visit destruction on the natives or their culture). It was also distinct from the "white martyrdom" of the highly ascetic desert fathers and mothers of Egypt. To be sure, many Irish monks were quite severe in their practices of mortification. Connolly names in particular the practice of "crosfigell," a term that migrated from the Latin *Crucis vigilia* and involved standing at great length in prayer with arms outstretched, cruciform.[27] Nevertheless, the green martyrdom represented a kind of earthy mixture of natural joy and practices aimed at spiritual growth.

If the natural landscape of Ireland and the social development of its Green Martyrs help explain the inviting spirituality of the monastery, then we still need to investigate the specific practices that gave rise to its ministry to penitents. And here the key practice is the tradition of monks having an *anamchara*, Gaelic for "soul-friend," who guided them in the spiritual life. The importance of this practice cannot be overstated. The *anamchara* was a spiritual guide, and each monk was expected to have such a person to whom they could "confess" their sins and from whom they would receive direction for growth in holiness and overcoming sin. The key practice between penitent and *anamchara* was "healing dialogue," which awakened the penitent to the possibility that "relationship with God could take the form of effective dialogue."[28] Ignoring this larger spiritual context, argues Connolly, is what leads to misreading the penitential texts as "mechanical and impersonal" laundry lists of sins and penances. As part of the dialogue, the *anamchara* would suggest penances. The penances were not aimed at "earning forgiveness," but rather were a form of "therapeutic sacrifice" designed to evoke awareness of dependence on God for mercy.[29]

In the healing dialogue, the monks were drawing on both indigenous and Christian sources. From their druid history, which had exalted the role of counselor, they embraced the ancient Irish adage that "anyone without a soul-friend is like a body without a head."[30] But the monks also drew on traditions of Eastern Christianity, which had come to them through monastic channels. According to Connolly, they were highly influenced by

27. Connolly, *Irish Penitentials*, 12.

28. Ibid., 14–16.

29. Ibid.

30. Ibid., 14.

the Desert Fathers and Mothers of the fourth century, "who engaged in the practice of *exagoreusis*, that is the opening of one's heart to another, which was believed to lead to *heyschia* or peace of heart."[31] The dialogical nature of penance in the monastery produced not only the Irish trademark of repeatable penance but also its clear connection with the restoration of health: the *anamchara* was seen as a skilled doctor, the sinner as a sick patient, and the penance as medicine. This theme was not original to them, and in fact is rooted in Christ's own understanding of his mission: "Those who are well do not need a physician, but the sick do, and I did not come to call the righteous but sinners" (Mark 2:17; Matt 9:12; Luke 5:31). The way in which the Irish monks embraced this mission led to interest from local villagers—and soon their *medicamenta penitentiae*, medicine of penance, became popular beyond the confines of the monastery.

In reading the history, one gets the sense that a key driver in the growth of Irish penance was the simple desire on the part of ordinary people to have someone listen to their struggles. In the older canonical system, a full and detailed manifestation of conscience was less emphasized, and thus, as Connolly notes, it was in Ireland that the term *confessio* began to be used to describe the process itself.[32] Of course, the medicine prescribed was not always easy, and we see here the danger of assuming that hard penances will push people away and lead to pastoral irrelevance. For example, church historian Ludwig Bieler reports that some local penitents were actually assigned to perform their long penances inside the monastery—in this sense, the monastic enclosure could become a kind of literal penitentiary.[33] As one group among many on the grounds—monks, students, workers, guests— penitents would be given special pastoral attention by an *anamchara*. Though their time there would include manual labor and ascetic practice, such hardships would be contextualized by the larger commitment of the monks to the penitents' bodily and spiritual health. Though it is not clear how often people were assigned to this kind of "incarceration," more common were cases when local people simply came to and from the monastery for ongoing dialogue with their *anamchara*. For this reason many commentators have referred to the Irish practice of confession as "spiritual direction," though it must be admitted, as we will soon see from the penances themselves, that it was a more demanding form of spiritual direction than

31. Ibid.

32. Ibid., 19.

33. Bieler, "Irish Penitentials," 332–33.

is common today. In any case, Bieler concludes that the Irish achieved a real development in ecclesial practice: "a change in the concept of penance from vindictive to remedial. . . . The emphasis shifts from atonement for sin to the moral rehabilitation of the sinner."[34]

The Penances of the Penitentials

I have just described the monastic context from which the Irish penitential tradition sprung. And the monks' commitment to the ongoing moral and spiritual reparation of the community—inside and outside the cloister—emerges clearly when we move to the crux of the topic at hand: an examination of the penitentials and the specific practices that they suggest. As noted, the penitentials are the texts that the monks developed in order to minister to penitents. Among the three great Irish texts, the earliest surviving document is *The Penitential of Finnian*, composed in the late 500s, followed by *The Penitential of Columbanus* (early 600s) and *The Penitential of Cummean* (mid-600s). *The Old Irish Penitential* is later than these three (compiled around 800) but is the only one written not in Latin but in Gaelic. The texts are not uniform in scope or details, but, as Connolly consistently notes, they do offer a basic trajectory of advice for the *anamchara*: how to open the heart of the penitent through questions, which penances to give in order to heal the heart, and how to free the heart after completion of the penance. Indeed, this process resonates with each of the main elements in my definition of penance—lament, responsibility, and repair.

The penitentials make clear that before the soul-friend can help God heal the heart, it first must be pierced by the contrition of the penitent. The very first lines of *The Penitential of Finnian* urge the sinner to "beat his breast and seek pardon from God" in order to be ready to "make satisfaction and so be whole."[35] Finnian's emphasis on contrition, expressed as "weeping and tears by day and night," echoes the classic formulation of St. Ambrose, in which the waters of tears are a reminder of our baptismal cleansing. *The Penitential of Cummean*, too, invokes the early church inclusion of tears as one way in which sins are forgiven. And while the monks urge contrition, they also recognize that neither sorrow nor the capacity for conversion is achieved by the individual on their own. Especially in a time when the monks were still encountering a local community undereducated

34. Ibid., 335.
35. In Connolly, *Irish Penitentials*, 125.

in the moral virtues, the *anamchara* was needed as an expert surgeon to help God pierce and open the heart of the sinner. *The Penitential of Columbanus* attests to the need for thorough examination, urging the dialogue to include not just the external manifestation of sin but also the *commotionibus animi*, distractions of the mind, that are the springs from which bad actions flow.[36] In this way, these penitential texts of the sixth and seventh centuries all emphasize moving the penitent to see the root causes of their sins and to experience the root emotion of lament that opens the way to repairing its damage.

Between lament and repair, though, is responsibility, and this is cultivated by the monks through their most common refrain: the sinner must *poenitere*, do penance. Along with prayer, a favorite penance prescribed by the Irish monks was fasting in its many forms—from meat, wine, sex, or gossip, to name a few. In fact, in many instances, the texts simply assume that to do penance means to fast. As we will see, penance is the means by which the individual carries responsibility in their heart and, literally, in their body. And yet along with *poenitere*, the penitentials consistently make reference to a wider goal: the sinner must *satis facere*, make whole, or at least make repaired, what was broken. In fact, the emphasis on satisfaction is so strong among the Irish that the absolution would conclude rather than begin the process of *poenitere* and *satis facere*. Of course, to the contemporary reader, the placement of forgiveness after the period of penance is the most remarkable difference from present practice. And we will see that the shift to immediate absolution in the Middle Ages did coincide with a less robust, certainly less public, practice of penances, though I will argue that immediate absolution need not have this effect.

In their emphasis on satisfaction, the monks refer not just to healing the penitent but to repairing the harm that the sin has caused to the community—especially the damage to victims. For example, *The Penitential of Cummean* guides the confessor in dealing with a very specific, and common, offense of the day:

> He who by a blow in a quarrel renders a man incapacitated or maimed shall take care of [the injured man's] medical expenses and shall make good the damages for the injury and shall do [the injured man's] work until he is healed, and [also] do penance for half a year.[37]

36. Ibid., 131
37. In McNeill and Gamer, *Medieval Handbooks of Penance*, 107.

Here we see the imperative to *satis facere*, making amends for the sake of the victim, joined to the injunction to *poenitere*, done for the sake of the sinner. The two are related, since reparation for the monks was not a utilitarian calculation but a set of practices aimed at inculcating the repentance necessary to restore right relationship. Thus, both penance and satisfaction, as construed by the monks, aimed at what Connolly says the *anamchara* most wanted to see in the penitent: "concrete external evidence of the inner change of heart."[38]

At times in the penitentials, we even see a more creative connection between the traditional act of fasting and practices of restoration. Using the idea of the *fructum penitentiae*, the fruit of penance—which refers to the money saved through fasting from expensive items like meat or wine—the monks advised penitents to put the savings at the service of repairing the common good. Sometimes the *fructum penitentiae* was to be given over to the priest-*anamchara*, and, in some instances, it would be used inside the monastery. In this sense, it was distinct from alms and from restitution. But the idea of reaping the material rewards of penance and frugality for social reconstruction was very common in the penitentials. Certainly we see it in specific cases of theft, where the savings of long penances could serve as a means of restitution, but we also see the concept in wider contexts. For example, when *The Penitential of Finnian* takes up the case of a lay penitent who has committed adultery, not only is abstinence from sexual intercourse invoked, but a year of fasting—including from all wine and meats—is to create a substantial fund from which can be drawn both alms for the poor and a proper *fructum penitentiae* to be handed over to the priest.[39] In this way, the monks made clear that every sin has ecclesial and public consequences, and paying these debts not only calls penitents to take the common good seriously but also encourages them to put "skin in the game" of repairing society's moral fabric. Here we see most clearly one of the three elements I have mined for the penitential ethic: taking responsibility for sin, and doing so in a way that requires moral agency and buy-in from the offenders.

A final note about the monks' approach to fasting is in order. I have tried to show that they were not prescribing fasting simply for its own sake; rather, they were connecting it to larger moral goals. Nonetheless, it is true

---

38. Connolly, *Irish Penitentials*, 137.

39. McNeill and Gamer, *Medieval Handbooks of Penance*, 94. See also Connolly, *Irish Penitentials*, 82.

that fasting is hardly absent from a single case taken up in the penitentials. And the details of the fasts are often emphasized: whether salt can be added to bread, or if milk is allowed in porridge (in both cases the answer was usually no). Any reader of the texts wonders how—and of course if—people fully completed these penances, especially when lengthy. Abstinence from sexual intercourse was also a common part of penance—and here it was in addition to already prescribed times of sexual abstinence, including at a minimum the forty days before Easter, the forty days after Pentecost, the forty days before Christmas, plus every Saturday (Mary), Sunday (Sabbath), Wednesday and Friday (ferial fast days). The practical conclusion is that either the Irish people were selectively efficient producers of large families, or we must acknowledge the gap between the penitential texts and popular observance of them. Nonetheless, in assessing the texts, it is important not to fall into the misleading stereotype that the monks were simply rigorist keepers of a harsh disciplinary system. Allowances for the condition of the penitent were quite common, as were dispensations for days of celebration. In fact, in one of the most interesting examples, *The Old Irish Penitential* offers this reversal of practice: "Anyone who fasts on a Sunday through carelessness or austerity does a week's penance on bread and water."[40] This curious penance, prescribing fasting for not feasting, at least shows that the heart of the penitential system was not self-mortification but proper relationship: to goods, to each other, to time, and to the God from whom all these come.

"Cure by Contraries"

We have just taken a glimpse into the kinds of penances given by the monks. These penances were ordered toward personal transformation (*poenitere*, fasting) and toward social reconstruction (*satis facere*, making whole). Now it is appropriate to assess the specific strategies they employed in prescribing certain penances for certain sins. In searching for a guiding rationale, the monks drew deeply on their own monastic spirituality, specifically the writings of John Cassian. Cassian, a monk writing in the early 400s who drew on the work of Evagrius and the desert fathers, had produced two highly influential texts, *The Institutes* and *The Conferences*, that were seminal to the style of monasticism begun by St. Benedict. The Irish were especially influenced by his frequent usage of spiritual battle metaphors. For

40. McNeill and Gamer, *Medieval Handbooks of Penance*, 159.

Cassian, the monk was a *miles Christi*, soldier of Christ, and the monastic community was an army. The Irish appropriated this language, appealing to the warrior spirit of the people and urging them to join not the *Fianna*, the Celtic army, but the *militia Christi*.[41] More to the penitential point, Cassian had emphasized the dangers of the eight principal vices and the possibility of their "cure by contraries." This approach, invoked by the monks as *contraria contrariis sanantur*, helps to show that the penitentials were not simply fixated on sin, but they were designed to probe the disordered performance of vice for indications of a counterstrategy. *The Old Irish Penitential* captures this approach richly:

> The venerable of Ireland have drawn up from the rules of Scripture a penitential for the annulling and remedying of every sin, both small and great. For the eight chief virtues, with their sub-divisions, have been appointed to cure and heal the eight chief vices, with whatsoever springs from them.[42]

Here, then, is the quintessential strategy of social repair practiced by the monks: the transformation of society through the inculcation of virtue. For the defeat of gluttony, cultivate temperance. Against avarice, prescribe generosity. To those prone to anger, counsel meekness. For penitents who despair, encourage joy. In cases of lust, train in continence. When envy rules, require benevolence. Versus pride, invoke fear of the Lord. And for sloth, order work!

Perhaps the best way to see this strategy in effect is to look at particular cases of selected vices. For habits of gluttony, the vice that often begins the eightfold list, the usual recommendation in *The Penitential of Columbanus* was a week consuming only bread and water. But here again we see the creative cultivation of the contrary virtue emerge among the Irish. *The Old Irish Penitential* suggests that in response to sins of overeating, the penitent should also be prescribed practices of "feasting the poor." In the text, the reason for feasting the poor (*fled do bochtaib* in the original Irish) is clearly to uproot from the glutton the self-centeredness that blinds them to their proper relationship to the goods of the earth intended for all in the proper proportion.[43] Moreover, gluttony is not construed by the monks as only related to food or material goods. In this category the monks also place excessive talking and gossip. Here the penance is usually silence,

41 Connolly, *Irish Penitentials*, 9.

42. Ibid., 37–38.

43. Ibid., 46.

which inculcates the habit of temperance in speech, but it was also at times coupled with the requirement to undo the harm one has caused to another's reputation. In this way, the cultivation of virtue as a response to vice serves not only to correct the sinner but to amend the social situation.

Another example will serve to display the characteristics of the cure by contraries strategy through which the monks sought to confront the interior and exterior dimensions of sin. The sin of stealing was treated as a species of avarice, and it brought multidimensional penances. This included not only fasting but also restitution. Finnian, in fact, demands that clerics who have stolen "must make four-fold restitution to the injured party."[44] The monk here is drawing on the story of Zacchaeus (Luke 19), who makes just such a vow that is accepted by Jesus. The emphasis on restitution, consistent in the penitentials, also draws on the legal traditions of pre-Christian Ireland. *Brehon* law, which took its name from the *brehons*, successors to the druids, whose system of justice prevailed for centuries, only finally succumbed to the British system in the seventeenth century. The monks admired the *brehons* and *brehon* law, and they used it as a model in their insistence on restitution. As Connolly notes, according to this ancient form of justice, the "principle of compensation" meant that restitution had to be "commensurate with the extent of the injury and the status of the injured party."[45] In keeping this dimension, the monks construed penance not as eluding justice but as deepening it—a point that I will emphasize when I examine contemporary methods of dealing with crime.

Murder and the Monks

The clearest example of penance mixing with criminal justice in Irish Christianity is the practice known as the *pietatis obsequia*, the servitude of responsibility. Monks would require this practice in the case of premeditated murder. Finnian applies this penance to clerics only, but Columbanus extends the practice to the laity. [46] After a period of exile to another community—perhaps a monastery where prayer, work, and fasting (from meat, wine, and any contact with weapons) would help transform the heart of the killer—the perpetrator would consult with the *anamchara*, who would

44. In ibid., 51

45. Ibid., 3.

46. See McNeill and Gamer, *Medieval Handbooks of Penance*, 91. See also Charles-Edwards, "Penitential of Columbanus," 221.

discern readiness for the next step. If affirmed, the penitent would establish a fund from personal savings, along with the money earned in labor and with what was saved by not buying meat and wine (since the exile of labor and fasting was at times prescribed for several years). With these funds, the penitent would make compensation to the kinsmen of the slain. If advancing in conversion, and if accepted by the kinsmen, the perpetrator would then go to the household of the victim's family and present himself for their service, taking on the duties of the *pietatis obsequia*, the filial piety and obedience that is owed to the heads of a household. In this case, the first thing owed was the productive manual labor that the dead victim could no longer contribute. Thus, the penance clearly was aimed at remedying the material situation of the victim's family. This requirement of compensatory labor came to the monks through *brehon* law, in which the practice was called the *Goire*, the warming. The idea seems to be that if the victim's family can benefit from the penitent perpetrator's labor, and if that can help them somehow tolerate being in his presence, then the relationships involved can "thaw" and be directed toward healing.

Here, then, we see in fascinating detail how the monks adopted this Irish practice for the Christian purpose of promoting forgiveness. Of course, the forgiveness here is not seen as valuable only for the spiritual good of individuals—the categories of "private/public" and "spiritual/practical" should not be retrojected onto the monks—but was deeply tied to material needs of the community. For example, Finnian makes clear that part of the *pietatis obsequia* is the duty of care for the old.[47] Envisioned here is the case in which the loss of a highly productive son or husband leaves aging survivors indigent, and the manual labor and ongoing material care provided by the perpetrator becomes, oddly though it must have seemed, a kind of safety net. Moreover, cases of murder were often ensconced in a landscape of inter-familial disputes and tribal rivalries; this is probably why Colambanus makes clear that the *pietatis obsequia* is especially relevant for the laity. And the proclivity of these disputes to produce more victims also explains another practical benefit of the practice, namely, its role in preventing violent revenge by weaving perpetrators and victims into an interdependent pattern of relationship. In this way, as Connolly notes, the *pietatis obsequia* was invoked by the monks in order to "break the cycle of sin and to foment real reconciliation."[48]

47. McNeill and Gamer, *Medieval Handbooks of Penance*, 91.
48. Connolly, *Irish Penitentials*, 64.

In the case of murder, the monks clearly show their preference for interpersonal engagement as a driving dimension of penance and social repair. And even if their overall strategy was sound, we need not conclude that specific practices, like the *pietatis obsequia*, were perfect in their implementation. Ludwig Bieler notes that, while a long period of pre-restitution exile—Finnian has it at ten years, Colambanus at three years—may have been spiritually helpful to all involved, it was not entirely well suited to the material needs of the survivors, some of whom might even be dead when the perpetrator returns.[49] In this sense, Bieler argues that the monks were, at times, clumsy in their appropriation of *brehon* legal justice, although one could imagine a monk requiring payments to victims' families even during the exile. In any case, Bieler does acknowledge that, over time, the Irish became more adept at negotiating a spiritual-legal response to crime. In *The Old Irish Penitential*, for cases of murder, "provision is even made for a cooperation of the civic and ecclesiastical authorities," enabling a strong penitential dimension to punishment.[50] Bernhard Poschmann takes the point even further, arguing that, while references are made to external authorities, for the most part the monks saw themselves as dispensers of public justice: penitential law *was* penal law.[51] To make his point clear, Poschmann notes repeated references in the texts to the phrase *iudice sacerdote*, the judging role of the priest. My own view is that, while ecclesial and secular realms cannot simply be conflated, what is clear in the texts—and most relevant to the topic at hand—is that the monks seek to impose significant social expectations on those who have committed serious crimes. These penances were at one and the same time a pastoral strategy of rehabilitation for killers as well as a public system of compensation for victims' families. Seen in the context of the need in the ancient world to manage the dangers of violent crime, even Bieler concludes that the Irish monks help push forward a shift from "vindictive" punishment to "remedial" penance.[52]

One lingering question to raise at this point is the monks' response to killing in war. Then as now, the line between murder and war was thin—how to distinguish a killing committed for a personal reason, a family reason, a tribal reason, or some of each? On the surface of the matter, the penitentials are largely silent. Connolly can find only one instance of it, in a later text,

---

49. Bieler, "Irish Penitenitals," 337.

50. Ibid., 338. See also McNeill and Gamer, *Medieval Handbooks of Penance*, 166.

51. Poschmann, *Penance*, 128.

52. Bieler, "Irish Penitenitals," 335.

and the penance for killing in war is a fast of forty days. This relatively light penance, alongside the general silence, indicates to him an awareness of the "conflicting values which are at issue in a time of war" and thus a basic stance of "leniency."[53] Perhaps Connolly is right, but there is another way to interpret the silence of the texts, one that does not read into them our own preference for hardening the distinction between war and murder. That is, perhaps the monks were silent on the "issue" of war because it was not a separate category the monks used to analyze killing. Perhaps what we would now call "war" was, in fact, treated as part of the violent network of tribal and group killings with which they were very much concerned. And references do abound to penances involving the systematic renunciation of weapons.[54] Thus, the species of violence now named "war" may well have been within the purview of their penitential system, though this cannot be known for certain from the available evidence.

In chapter 5, I will compare the approach in the penitentials to contemporary responses to crime. No doubt, some of the features of today's challenges will be different, but it is important to pause and appreciate what relevance there is in the penitentials. First, as noted, the world that the Irish monks inherited was riven by violence and tribal enmity. Even if, as Cahill suggests, the monks were highly effective trainers in the way of nonviolence, the frequent references to murder in the penitentials reveal that this was a common problem—for monks and clerics as well as laity. Thus, we cannot interpret the monks as writing for a utopian society, different in essence from our own "real world." Second, while today the religious practice of confession is entirely separate from legal processes for one who has committed a crime, the Irish confessor-as-judge presents a relevant model. In fact, in addition to the term *anamchara* (soul-friend), the penitentials refer to the *animadversor* (soul-adversary). To perform this role well, the confessor needed not only to assign physical penances and satisfactions—"do this, go there, pay that"—but to provide spiritual direction as well. *The Penitential of Cummean* reminds the *animadversor* to "carefully observe" the context of the crimes: the level of "learning" of the sinner, their "afflictions" and "oppressions."[55] This judicial diligence did not lead to light penances, but it did place the role of judge in a holistic context. And this construal of the judicial role will be helpful in making contemporary applications.

53. Connolly, *Irish Penitentials*, 66.

54. See McNeill and Gamer, *Medieval Handbooks of Penance*, 94.

55. Ibid., 117.

While a judge or jury today rules on the body of the defendant—it is in fact the *habeus corpus* ("present the body") principle that brings the suspect to them—the *animadversor* takes responsibility also for the sinner's soul. In closing his penitential, Cummean even reminds the confessor-judge that his own "reward," "satisfaction," and "glory" are tied to the sinner's reformation.[56] In this way, as I will argue more fully in chapter 5, the Irish monks are offering elements that can contribute to a real alternative model in courts and penitentiaries today.

Taking Responsibility: Penance as Punishment

As noted, critiques of Irish reconciling practices often begin by describing their system as "private." In response, I have tried to demonstrate the thoroughly public dimensions of their practice. Certainly, while the healing dialogue of confession is best described as a personal, one-to-one conversation in the tradition of spiritual direction, there was nothing private about the performance of penance and reconciliation in the societies surrounding the monasteries. In this final section, I will highlight the element of interpersonal responsibility as a key contribution of the Irish monks to an ethic of social repair. To begin, I wish to address a critique of their system related to the "private" charge. Many histories associate the Irish with a system of *tariff penances* in which every sin had its price—and the payment of such tariffs was open for negotiation.[57] In such a construal, as Ladislas Orsy puts it, "all remained hidden, a secret transaction between the priest and the penitent."[58] What could be interpersonal about this approach?

It is true that over time the monks used the Latin term *arreum*, equivalent price, to signify the value of a penance.[59] And often monetary alms were used as a kind of tariff to be paid as part of penance. Noneconomic equivalents were also allowed in ascetic practice. One such *arreum* that could replace a yearlong fast was a *Triduanum* comprised of three days without food and with just a few sips of water, along with recitation of psalms and periods of standing *crosfigell*.[60] The eighth-century document known as *An Old Irish Table of Commutations* is clear that the point here is

56. Ibid.
57. Poschmann, *Penance*, 127.
58. Orsy, *Evolving Church*, 35.
59. Bieler, "Irish Penitentials," 335.
60. See Poschmann, *Penance*, 127.

to intensify the penitential process, not elude it.[61] If substantive concession was made, it was only in cases such as an ill or elderly penitent who gives alms or prays in place of a bodily fast. Still, when exported from Ireland, the tables of commutation led to practices such as penance by proxy. In a case from tenth-century England, an elite penitent hires a team of men to help him complete a seven-year penance in three days.[62] Thus, there may be some truth to the claim that the Irish opened the way for a transactional model of penance to emerge later. However, in the way the Irish themselves put a tariff or "price" on sin, we can see evidence of the emphasis on responsibility. As Poschmann notes, the concept of *arreum* is economic and related to the idea in Celtic brehon practice of ensuring restitution. By putting a "price" on sin, the monks thus helped reinforce the value of the victims and the common good. Far from letting offenders off the hook, this system required, to use words from my definition of penance, *taking responsibility for* the wounds and damages caused by sin. This responsibility was individual, but also shared: Irish confessors on occasion even took on a portion of the penitent's hardship. What might seem here like another concession in fact emerges from the *anamchara*'s role as "fellow-sufferer," inscribing them into the interpersonal repair work.[63] Thus, despite later developments, Poschmann affirms that for the Irish penance was never "a mechanical business."[64]

With an emphasis on taking responsibility a clear theme for the Irish, I can now suggest that their penitential practices might offer some ways to construe the work of punishment. We moderns think of punishment as something dispensed by a judge, but the Irish add two models worthy of note: the navigator and the doctor. As I noted, for the most serious sins, including murder, one of the many requirements imposed on the culprit was exile—banishment to another place. But the monks saw this as a pilgrimage, a *peregrinatio*, to "another city."[65] What drives this is not the need for expulsion. To be sure, there are rare references to *peregrinatio perennis*, permanent relocation to the domain of another monastery and a different *anamchara*. But "another city" signifies not just a physical relocation but a new moral terrain where a new set of relationships and a fresh revival

---

61. See McNeill and Gamer, *Medieval Handbooks of Penance*, 142–47.

62. Poschmann, *Penance*, 128.

63. Connolly, *Irish Penitentials*, 182.

64. Poschmann, *Penance*, 128–29.

65. McNeill and Gamer, *Medieval Handbooks of Penance*, 91.

of virtue is possible. What matters most is not where "another city" is, but whether the hardship of being sent there—which is a kind of punishment—provides re-orientation for the one who has gone astray and is in need of an *anamchara* as navigating guide.[66]

A related notion emerges in the way the monks use a doctor-patient relationship to understand penance as medicine. For the monks, the question about punishment is not "is it hard enough to fit the crime?" but rather "is it designed to fit the cure?" And the cure was understood as health not only for the culprit but for the community—a process so important it was considered the central task of monk-*anamchara*s to oversee. As Cummean himself puts it, the penitential vocation of monks is "the health-giving medicine of souls," which through "treatments" aims at "the remedy of wounds."[67] What is most remarkable about the Irish construal of punishment is the way that the judicial, medical, and pilgrimage models complement each other. The insistence on justice and restitution prevents the medicine of penance from being merely a therapeutic, self-directed placebo. The reorientation sought in the pilgrimage model presses for a sense of justice that is not retributive but restorative. And the way in which medicine must take account of needs in the human condition renders pilgrim penitents more fortified for their difficult journey.

In chapter 1, I defined penance as the practices through which persons lament, take responsibility for, and seek to repair the wounds that are caused by sin. Clearly, the penances preferred by the Irish monks reflect this threefold purpose. The interpersonal encounter between offender and *anamchara* was precisely directed to lament and responsibility, "piercing and opening the heart," as the monks put it. It is the centrality of those dialogues that has led many to see the system as private and individual, but what this misses is that these exchanges were also directed toward the third element in my definition of penance: the repair of wounds. The monks did not forget that the wounds inside of offenders also have social significance, and a robust commitment to healing them is not in competition with attention to the wounds of victims. In fact, the two are tied. And before we criticize the Irish monks for inaugurating a system of penance that gives seeming disproportionate one-to-one attention to sinners and even violent criminals, we should consider not only their insistence on satisfaction and making amends but also their success. That is, on the level of pure historical

66. See Connolly, *Irish Penitentials*, 177–80.
67. McNeill and Gamer, *Medieval Handbooks of Penance*, 99.

assessment, no one doubts that the monks were enormously effective in their endeavor to change Irish society. The fact that they engaged a factionalized society and created a far less violent culture, one devoid of human sacrifice and with an impressive commitment to arts and letters—and all this through a nonviolent evangelization that avoided the martyrdom so common elsewhere—should lead us to pause and consider the value of their approach to social repair.

In particular, the Irish monks offer two promising resources. First, the penitential practices enmeshed in Ireland's monastic communities of the fifth to ninth centuries were designed to facilitate multiple layers of responsibility and relationship among offenders, victims, and society. Second, such practices reveal a commitment to the principle that the response to crime should not be to remove individual moral agency from those directly involved but rather to promote it—so long as it is exercised under the direction of responsible guides. As we will see, this Irish principle exemplifies a classic axiom of Catholic social doctrine: subsidiarity. That is, the more levels of interpersonal engagement involved in the work of re-establishing right relationship, the deeper the social repair. In the case of the Irish monks, this principle was quite effective in holding together a commitment to victims, to the community at large, and to offenders themselves. I will not be so bold as to suggest that through their penitential tradition the Irish can "save civilization" again, but the practices that have been on display in this chapter do deserve to be mined as a resource in the present and pressing task of finding alternatives to our criminal justice strategies.

3

A *Summa* for the Americas:
Thomas Aquinas and Reparation

KIMBERLY THEIDON, THE HARVARD anthropologist who has spent much of her academic career writing about the legacy of suffering left by the civil war in Peru, concludes that "my experiences in Peru have convinced me that the work of postconflict social repair involves reconstructing the human."[1] In societies long torn by conflict, the challenge is that the *re*-construction actually is not referential to some healthy past but to the possibility of a *new future*. And if this future is to become real, those who have survived a conflict—victims, perpetrators, bystanders—will need to find creative resources to build something not only authentically human but also authentically new. In my introductory chapter, I described what is needed as a "horizon of hope," and Thomas Aquinas, I will argue in this chapter, is a key resource in helping wounded communities seek it.

First, I will briefly set the context for the period of penitential theology that came before him—a period that spans from the monastic practices of the previous chapter to the "synthesis" regarding the sacrament that occurred at the Fourth Lateran Council in 1215. Then I will explicate Aquinas' treatment of penance, focusing on the context of justice and on his distinction between restitution and satisfaction. An illustrative example then follows of how Aquinas' principles were and were not employed by Dominicans trying to resist the conquest of the Americas. To conclude, I will offer some preliminary points of contemporary application, a task that will be more fully developed in chapter 6, in which I take up the continuing crisis of truth and reconciliation in Peru.

1. Theidon, *Intimate Enemies*, 54.

From the Monastery to the Confessional

Moving from the penitential practices of the Irish monks to the theological paradigm of St. Thomas Aquinas is a jump of several centuries and a shift to a very different world and church context. As I have stated, my aim is not to provide a history of the sacrament of penance, and I am self-consciously highlighting the three sources that I see as crucial bridges from Christian theology to political practice. Moreover, I want to resist a facile narration of history that sees the early Middle Ages as a period of simple decline and privatization in the penitential practices of the church. In fact, several interesting examples in this period are worth retrieving and gleaning for their potential resonance today. Thus, before moving into the main resource for this chapter, Aquinas, I want to highlight a few of those developments.

Perhaps the most provocative innovation in this period—and certainly relevant to the problem of criminal justice raised in the last chapter—comes from the *Gelasian Sacramentary*, probably compiled in Paris during the mid-700s. It contains a provision that calls for the incarceration of certain serious sinners, whether clerical or lay. Poschmann notes that not only this text but others prescribe in certain cases of murder, adultery, and perjury that "the penitent is to be kept in confinement from the beginning of his penance on Ash Wednesday until Maundy Thursday."[2] He notes that "the essential point was the detection and punishment of criminals, and the control of their penance in custody, whether in the bishops' residence or in their own dwelling-place," though it also squared with earlier practices by which people "were frequently consigned to a monastery to do penance."[3] If incarceration sent a strong signal, then so, too, did the elaborate rituals for reception back into the community, with the penitent lying prostrate on Holy Thursday and a deacon pleading his cause to the bishop, who then welcomed him with the laying on of hands and embraced him in front of the faithful—a process, even without incarceration, that has had remarkable lasting power from the early practices of the church to the present-day reinvigoration of Lent.

On the matter of incarceration and control of reformation, we can note corollaries to elements of Irish practice and to the aforementioned concept of a "penitentiary." This illustrates not only the intermingling of civil and religious law in early medieval society but also the reluctance of

---

2. Poschmann, *Penance*, 137.
3. Ibid.

the church to lose the critical task of penitential repair in response to crime. Of course, the promise of a return to the original purposes of a penitentiary has a dark side well worth remembering. The Orthodox Church in Russia, for example, used monasteries for the incarceration of church and state criminals, beginning under Imperial Russia in 1441 and ending only in 1905.[4] The stories that emerged—of persecution for dissent, or horrific treatment and isolation—are a sober reminder that the point here is to mine the church's theological tradition carefully. Facile suggestions that the church knows best how to conduct the reform of individuals must be met with such cautionary tales. Thus, we can simply note that in the early Middle Ages, the church in the West still saw the reformation of criminals as within its purview and mission. Even as political societies in the Middle Ages began to integrate and institutionalize, with ecclesial practices of penance becoming less public, the church was still offering resources for this task—especially in moral philosophy, theology and the sacraments.

The other development to note in the centuries after Irish penitential practice is that the form of a person-to-person sacramental encounter became the norm in the church. Nathan Mitchell points out that the social dimension of reparation does fall away to an extent, and the act of confession becomes the penitential experience.[5] And from the year 950, rules for confession in liturgical texts begin to specify that absolution be given immediately upon confession.[6] As we saw, the usual practice of the Irish monks called for the word of forgiveness to be given at the end of the process. But, while penance thus becomes—at least in practical operation—a kind of consequence of the reconciling sacrament, it still remains an important element within its construal. In fact, just what elements constitute the sacrament became the major focus of debate during this period and led church leaders to formalize the practice within the official ministry of the church. This happens in 1215 at the Fourth Lateran Council, convoked by Pope Innocent III.

This Lateran Council, which brings us to the decade before Aquinas is born, is a significant development for the practice of confession. One major move at Lateran is to stress the priestly role in the sacrament, which results from what tradition called *the power of the keys* to bind and loose sins (Matt 16:19; 18:18, 20). But this was more than a legal dictate, since the Council

4. See Shubin, *Monastery Prisons*.

5. Mitchell, *Rite of Penance*, 35.

6. Dallen, *Reconciling Community*, 115.

also stressed that confessors practice the "art of arts" and must be well-prepared as guides. To this end, Raymond of Penaforte wrote a popular *Summa* for confessors, stressing the care for souls involved in hearing confessions—an idea strongly resonant with the Irish role of the *anamchara*. He also insisted on distinguishing the craft of discerning a penitent's sins and the power of absolving them. His distinction raises another feature of this period, which is that apparently, until this time, there had been at least some practice of lay confession, including to women—often, but not always, without absolution being given. Kate Dooley notes that some classic examples come from Ireland, with Saints Ita and Bridget, as well from other European women, like St. Fare, who held this role as part of being a monastic abbess. Moreover, she notes that many monastic rules, including the famous Rule of St. Basil, ascribe this role to women. The practice was apparently prevalent enough for Pope Innocent III to intervene and order it stopped in the case of the Cistercian monastery of Las Huelgas in Burgos, Spain.[7] For Dooley, the point here is that the diversely practiced forms of "manifestatio conscientiae" made clear that ongoing conversion and guidance in holiness were the needs that drove penitential practice.

At the Lateran Council, practices like lay confession became clearly heterodox. As Dallen notes, "The two ancient roles of spiritual counselor and community official were thus combined in the person of the priest-confessor."[8] Part of this standardization was to safeguard the integrity of the practice against evasion and other anomalies. The Council, for example, forbade people from moving from parish to parish for confession; it was one's local priest who should serve this role. Moreover, the Council instituted what came to be known as the "Easter Duty" of going to confession at least once a year in order to receive the Eucharist during Eastertime. Following the Lateran synthesis, confession also comes to be defined as one of seven sacraments, and many *Summas* arise that give it prominence and clarify its elements. Aquinas concurs in this synthesis but, as I will show, places penance in a wider scope, one replete with significance for social repair. There is but one inconvenient matter for me, though: it was mid-treatment of the subject of penance when Aquinas had a mystical experience and, as a result of the comparative insignificance of his writing—"it seems to me as so much straw"—stopped his project. Despite his suggestive

---

7. See Dooley, "Women Confessors," 271–81.

8. Dallen, *Reconciling Community*, 142.

experience, and devoid of that mystical grace, the rest of this chapter will explore what we can know of his approach to penance.

Aquinas, Justice, and Politics

What makes Aquinas so fruitful for my project can be described on two levels. First, the matter of the common good is never far from Aquinas' view, and, even in treating individual sins, we can see the way in which countervailing social virtues, especially justice, are omnipresent. Second, the principles of Aquinas have a long history of being applied to questions of communal repair. As I will show, his treatment of restitution became the central text guiding Christian resistance to conquest in the sixteenth century. For these general reasons, not to mention his overall stature in Catholic tradition, St. Thomas is a fitting source to explore in the task of assembling an ethic of social repair. More specifically, Aquinas can add an element of creativity to the way in which we construe reparation—moving it from a contested claim about how to remake the past toward an inviting vision for building a new future.

Living from 1225 to 1274, Aquinas came of age as a scholar during a time of rich intellectual discourse. The period from the eleventh to thirteenth centuries is known as the High Middle Ages, a time when art, culture, and scholarship were bringing synthesis to the societies of Europe. The move away from feudal, localized communities toward integrated polities marks what Aquinas scholar Jean Porter often calls an era of "proto-globalization." Of special importance in this period was the task of mining multiple traditions—from Aristotelian to early Christian to Islamic sources—for wisdom on the meaning of human nature and the scope of law. The institution that emerged to undertake the task of synthesis was the university. The dominant model in previous centuries had been the monastery, but Christian scholarship was now being practiced in a much more urban context, and the intellectual project became focused on classic texts and systematizing the mass of knowledge in these sources. Schools, in places like Bologna, Salerno, and Paris, began to draw students around an exciting proposition: the production of philosophy rooted in the intelligibility of the natural world. The schoolmen—we now call them Scholastics—who lectured in these burgeoning institutions were deeply committed to the capacity of human reason to draw common scientific and moral conclusions. In this way, Aquinas, who became the greatest of these Scholastics, saw no need to pit human reason and the moral capacities of human nature against the ultimate ends for which God made us.

A helpful, and classic, maxim in the interpretation of Aquinas is his own phrase, *gratia non tollit naturam sed perficit*, "grace perfects nature."[9] The work of God is not at odds with creation and human life; rather, grace affirms our natural goodness and deepens our capacity for virtue. Consider, for example, the difference between Aquinas and Peter Lombard, whose *Sentences* from the mid-twelfth century was the text that formed the basis for Aquinas' first major commentary as an apprentice professor at the University of Paris. Lombard devoted extensive attention to the theological virtues—faith, hope, and love—and very little to the cardinal—prudence, temperance, fortitude, and justice. And even then, he treats them as supernaturally infused, not as naturally acquired.[10] By contrast, Aquinas situates his treatment on the virtues with the bold claim that "human virtue directed to the good, which is defined according to the rule of reason, can be caused by human acts."[11] In other words, through rational deliberation and through the practice of habituation, human beings can acquire virtue. Aquinas then immediately affirms the dictum of St. Augustine that there are virtues "which God works in us without us," since they are infused through grace and ordered to a supernatural end.[12] The debates over the relationship of nature and grace in Aquinas are classic and still at full throttle. For now, I simply want to note that Aquinas construed natural virtue as a human good, understandable to reason, and attainable by all people. This commitment, rooted in Aristotle and ancient philosophy, has drawn Catholics and secularists alike to return to Aquinas for insights regarding contemporary and shared moral challenges like social repair.

If Aquinas provides resources for reflection on properly political challenges facing the human community, then and now, then the appropriate place to begin is with the most important resource that he proposes to any polity: the practice of virtue. And, of the four cardinal virtues, by far the longest treatment in the *Summa theologiae* is devoted to justice. Indeed, it is within the virtue of justice that Aquinas treats the virtue of penance. Aquinas defines justice as "a constant and perpetual will rendering *ius suum unicuique*, to each his due."[13] This definition follows closely the concept

9. Aquinas, *Summa theologiae* (ST), I-I, 1.8, ad 2.

10. See Bushlack, "Justice in the Theology of Thomas Aquinas," 146–50.

11. ST I-II, 63.2.

12. Ibid.

13. Ibid., II-II 58.1.

of Cicero and the philosophical tradition, giving the virtue clear political currency and distinguishing it from that which is given to others for different reasons, for example, in charity. This concept of justice, however, is more expansive than it might at first seem. Cicero's original formulation describes justice as "a habit of the mind, preserving the common interest, and assigning *ius suum cuique*, to each one his due."[14] Thus, even from the start, the "justice as due" concept has in it a wide canvass of practices serving the common good and promoting right relationships. Moreover, the word "due" here (*ius* for Aquinas, *dignitatem* for Cicero) should not so easily be restricted only to what we call "rights." Mutual obligations can easily take us beyond what political entities deem as rights. This point will become important for my project, since debates over reparation often get mired in the question of what people "have a right to," rather than what is fitting for personal and communal flourishing.

William Mattison advances this point in suggesting that when Aquinas uses a term like "ius suum unicuique," we should not be satisfied with a simple definition like "to each his due" or "to each his right." Rather, according to Mattison, "*ius* refers to the 'proper order of things,' or 'the way things were meant to be.' It is a state of affairs marked by peace, or harmony, since there exist genuine right relations with others. The just person seeks such a state in all her acts."[15] Here we see the concept of justice as right relationship come fully into view. And the reason that Mattison can claim that this more expansive sense of *ius* is at work is the broad substantive ground that Aquinas covers as he proposes what justice involves. In describing justice as the virtue that directs all human action toward the common good, Aquinas specifies that the common good is more important than and not equivalent to the sum of individual goods in a society.[16] In this sense, we see that justice cannot be a simple collection of *dues* owed this or that person, though it includes them. Rather, justice is the virtue that arranges the proper *order* of communal life. For this reason, it is not just the private interests or claims of affected parties, but rather the concern for the presence and vitality of justice itself that should drive a community to establish and re-establish right relationships among its people. On the primacy of the common good, Aquinas follows Aristotle, who argued that the good of the *polis* is "the

14. Cicero, *De Inventione* III, c.53, in Bushlack, "Justice in the Theology of Thomas Aquinas," 147.

15. Mattison, *Introducing Moral Theology*, 136.

16. See ST II-II 47.10 ad 2 and II-II 58.7.ad 2.

greater and more perfect thing to attain and to safeguard."[17] The reason is that a *polis* that practices and can inculcate virtue, across time and space, moves toward a universal, comprehensive, and ultimately divine good—in which individuals can participate and enjoy true happiness.

This understanding of the common good is quite relevant today, highlighting the need to purify the meaning of justice in societies where the ability to assert self-interest drives politics. Such is the case, as we will see, in Peru, where the voices of victim-survivors of the civil war are still not being heard in their calls for restoration. What is at stake, thus, is not only rights, and not even the actual lot of those victims, but also the future of the whole society in its ability to form virtuous and flourishing persons. A people cannot live with consistently disordered relationships among them and still thrive morally. In his classic book *The Four Cardinal Virtues*, Joseph Pieper makes an interesting observation along these lines regarding justice in the *Summa*. He begins with a question, asking why Aquinas defines justice in reference to that which is already one's own, *suum unicuique*. Pieper responds that hidden in this concept is a "surprise formulation" that Aquinas felt unnecessary to state in the definition but that is critical to understanding his project. This unstated premise, according to Pieper, is that, even to speak of justice, we must face squarely "the startling fact that a man may *not* have what is nonetheless 'his own'—as the very concept of 'something due a person implies.'"[18] That is, Aquinas is reminding us *in his very definition of justice* that we must be on the lookout for those who do not have what in fact ought to be their own. In this way, justice is not about preserving some already existing social order, let alone our own place within it, but about seeking the constant re-establishment of relationship with those alienated from "their due." And in this endeavor, Pieper reminds us "that man, especially, is just who does not become inured and hardened to disorder," which, even in the best societies, is all around us.[19] Indeed, an important antidote to the kind of cynicism and self-interest that can dominate politics is the continual reassertion—on full display in Aquinas—that justice can only be found in relationship.

17. Aristotle, *Nichomachean Ethics*, 1094b, 4.

18. Pieper, *Four Cardinal Virtues*, 79.

19. Ibid., 80.

Restitution and the Image of God

Restitution is the practice that, for Aquinas, drives the re-establishment of justice after wrongdoing. It involves restoring to victims the material goods that have been taken, but also restoring their ability to possess, direct, and manage those goods and their lives. This human capacity to direct, which he calls *dominium*, is invoked at the very beginning of Aquinas' treatment of restitution. "To restore" the goods that have been taken is "the same as to reinstate a person in the possession or *dominium*" of them.[20] So important is the term that Aquinas uses it to assert that the human being is "master of his actions through his reason and will"—that is, he is *dominus* of his acts, just as God is *Dominus* of creation.[21] Put another way, as the image of God, we have the power to rationally direct our goods and our actions for specific purposes and ends. Later interpreters, such as Francisco Vitoria, use this principle as the basis for an expansive view of restitution as restoring not just goods but persons.

In Aquinas' massive treatment of the particular practices of justice, which number well over fifty, restitution comes first. After his opening treatment, just outlined, Aquinas takes up some specific test cases about when and how and by whom restitution must be made. One question he takes up is how to make restitution in those cases when life or limb cannot be restored. Aquinas argues that there must be "compensation either in money or in honor" and that for adjudication of what is due, the community can rely on "the judgment of a good man."[22] And to whom should restitution be made when the victim is dead? Here he is clear that restitution is to be granted to "the heir, who is looked upon as one" with the victim.[23] Interestingly, Aquinas here also suggests that, in cases when the precise identity of victims is not known, restitution must be made through "alms" directed toward the common good. Alms here does not refer to gratuitous charity, since, for Aquinas, this is a distinct virtue, but rather to an act of restitution to society, and this option is only relevant after "a careful inquiry" into the identity of the victim. [24] Even if the victims are later discovered to be dead, the material aid given for the common good of the community, especially

20. ST II-II 62.1.

21. Ibid., I-II 1.1. See Brett, *Liberty, Right and Nature*, 16.

22. Ibid., II-II 62.2.

23. Ibid., II-II 62.5.

24. Ibid.

the poor, will serve the "spiritual welfare" of the deceased as well as approximate a just act of restitution.[25]

I am aware that Aquinas does not have in mind here the kind of massive social reparation paradigms often recommended by truth and reconciliation commissions. Nevertheless, his treatment of justice simply cannot be read as only applying to disputes between singular, private individuals. In fact, undergirding Aquinas' treatment of justice are two things: an assumption about the thoroughly political nature of restitution and an argument about the importance of it as a matter of public law. As Aquinas himself argues, "Man has a natural aptitude for virtue, but the perfection of virtue must be acquired by means of some kind of training."[26] One important source for this training comes through law. In her book *Ministers of the Law*, Porter claims that, on this point, Aquinas was quite keen to vindicate Aristotle's account of people as "political animals" whose "orderly pursuit of common goals" requires giving "a central place to the polity, that is to say, to a community structured through and sustaining the political activities of its members."[27] In this way, the role of political authority in ensuring the justice of restitution is twofold. Not only ought it to protect victims by curbing the vice of ignoring the harm done to their *dominium* and dignity, but it ought to teach and promote virtue by ordering and facilitating the process of restitution in society.

Actually, the government's role in restitution is broader still, because Aquinas also implicates government as one of the agents often responsible not only for monitoring restitution but for *making* it. As the conclusion to his treatment of restitution, Aquinas asks if only the one who has done harm to a victim is bound to make restitution. Aquinas says no. His reason is that cooperation with an injustice can also bring responsibility for the injustice. We do well to note his precise moves here, since the question of cooperation with evil came to dominate penitential theology in the late medieval and early modern era. Aquinas says that one can become a cooperator directly—through encouragement, praise, or material assistance for a wrongdoer—or one can play a role indirectly—through silence and not counseling against the act. Aquinas admits that not all cases of cooperation demand restitution, but he notes several that do demand it in every instance. Included in this category are, of course, those who actually assist

25. Ibid.

26. Ibid., II-I 95.1.

27. Porter, *Ministers of the Law*, 141.

in crimes that need cooperation to be committed. But he goes further: "Persons in authority who are bound to safeguard justice on earth, are bound to restitution, if by their neglect thieves prosper, because their salary is given to them in payment of their preserving justice here below."[28] He does note that if the perpetrators of a crime—those who are the "commanders" and "executors" of it—make restitution, then the political officials are no longer liable, since the point of restitution for Aquinas is not chiefly punitive but, rather, restorative for the victim. But when restitution is not made by the principals, the responsibility of those in authority is heightened, "in virtue of their office."[29]

Aquinas' treatment of the need for a public role in monitoring and making restitution does not even assume the case in which the government *is* the principal actor in wrongdoing. In such a case restitution is demanded not simply by the just-mentioned logic of public authority, but by its status as perpetrator. This point is not insignificant to make when dealing with situations like Peru during the civil war where military members, agents of public authority responsible for the common good, were engaged in oppression, violence, and mass killing. Of course, as we will see, military leaders in Peru made and make a classic response to charges of culpability and demands for restitution. Killing, even if sometimes the killing of innocent persons, is an unavoidable consequence in the effort to protect the common good and rid society of a terrorist threat. Aquinas explicitly rejects this logic. Killing the innocent is always wrong. In fact, considering a person "in relation to himself," with a human nature created by God, he admits it is wrong to kill anyone whatever the cirucumstances.[30] "In relation to the common good," he supports the ability of political authority to execute criminals and to kill unjust aggressors who are a threat to the community.[31] Still, he never neglects the need for political leaders to investigate guilt or innocence. Even when ordered by a judge, for instance, a subject should not execute one he knows to be innocent—though it is true that, in cases involving lower-level officials, Aquinas mitigates their culpability.[32] But not in this case, nor in any case, does Aquinas hedge on the restitution owed

---

28. ST II-II 62.7.
29. Ibid., II-II 62.7 ad 2.
30. Ibid., II-II, 64.6.
31. Ibid., II-II 40.1 and 64.2.
32. See ibid., II-II 64.6 ad 3.

to those who are unjustly harmed or killed, even when this occurs at the hands of public authorities.

In sum, Aquinas' treatment of restitution yields a practice aimed at restoration after injustice. The practice is aimed at restoring victims to their personal dignity as well as re-establishing the whole society's pursuit of justice. In this way, restitution is both natural to human beings' political nature and at the same time necessary for growth in virtue and holiness. As a political practice, restitution manifests society's concern for victims and its respect for law—law not in the positivist sense but in the natural sense. Indeed, Porter notes that, for Aquinas, the natural law is not an external rule set foisted on us but rather our shared rational capacity to seek good, avoid evil, and order our lives toward personal and communal ends—the very ends outlined in Aquinas' treatment of justice.[33] Put another way, civil law should promote restitution because it corresponds to the natural law operative within us. This law is evident in and expressed through a desire for social repair after experiences of injustice. Theologically, Aquinas makes clear that restitution is tethered to the ultimate end of human life: union with God. Thus he argues, echoing Augustine on this point, that "since the safeguarding of justice is necessary for salvation, it follows that it is necessary for salvation to restore what has been taken unjustly."[34] Here we see the way in which the treatment of restitution exhibits the principle of grace perfecting nature. Just as throughout the *Summa* there is no minimization of natural virtues, nor a collapse of them under the weight of supernatural ends, so too there is no eclipse of properly political practices like restitution—even when, as we will see, he presents his theology of penance.

Aquinas after the Conquest

Aquinas' concept of justice, which, by its very definition, focused on those deprived of what ought to be *suum cuique*, their own—their goods, their *dominium*, their dignity—and the privileged place he gave to restitution made his work ripe for employment in a situation of deep social injustice. The most notable figure to do just that was Bartolomé de Las Casas, in the sixteenth century. A priest who had himself been part of the Conquest of the Americas, Las Casas gradually became aware of the oppressive reality of the New World and sought out the resources of Catholic tradition to

33. See Porter, "Virtue of Justice," 278–79.

34. ST II 62.2.

fight against it. Aquinas' *Summa,* and in particular its treatment of restitution, became a key resource as he sought to convince all—from kings to churchmen to conquistadores—that the urgent task of their day was to dismantle the injustice of the Conquest, repair its wounds, and build a truly new world.

In emphasizing the depth of injuries in the New World, Las Casas invokes the provocative idea that justice requires the Spaniards to move "ultra restitutionem ad satisfactionem," beyond restitution to satisfaction.[35] The term *satisfaction* has deep roots in the Christian penitential tradition. The Irish monks, as we saw, emphasized the need to *satis facere,* to make whole, what had been broken. For them, satisfaction indicated a particularly robust and full form of restitution—like paying all the medical bills of someone wrongly injured, or doing years of labor for the family of someone slain. Practices such as prayer, fasting, and pilgrimage accompanied the imperative to *satis facere,* working together to transform the heart of the penitent and repair the rupture to communal life. Of course, the place where this process was inaugurated, reviewed, and ratified was in the sacramental encounter of penitent and guide. We do not know how familiar Las Casas was with the early practices of the monks, but he seems to prefer many elements of their model over the prevailing practice of his day—including the sense that reparation *precedes* forgiveness. Las Casas had witnessed the Dominican practice of *refusing* absolution and concluded that it could be an effective way to inculcate true penitence and pursue desperately needed social repair. And so, when he became the bishop of Chiapas, he began to recommend this strategy to the priests of his diocese. In 1553, he published the plan in *Confesionario,* which Gustavo Gutiérrez notes "is one of his most controversial books and one of those that caused him the most trouble in his life."[36] In the text, the bishop offers twelve rules that apply when conquistadores, *encomenderos,* or merchants of slaves and weapons come for confession.

Rule number one for Las Casas is that the penitent must want to "stand before the judgment seat of God" and give the confessor total power to determine the extent of the restitution, even if the priest "should judge it necessary for the man to give back all he owns . . . leaving nothing at all to his heirs."[37] The reason that such restitution could be possible, of course, is

---

35. Casas, *De unico vocationis modo* 7, §5.

36. Gutiérrez, *Las Casas,* 365.

37. Casas, *Confesionario,* 282.

that, for Las Casas, anything that the person gained through dealings in the Americas is a form of robbery of the goods, both material and "the things more precious," that were the proper dominium of the natives.[38] It is the job of the confessor to determine objectively the extent of that robbery with which the penitent was involved and the precise nature of the restitution. In addition to the possibility that the priest will require the penitent to divest his entire financial portfolio to pay for the restitution, the sinner must also agree to free any slaves he holds. As Las Casas bluntly puts it, "He is to give them their freedom instantaneously, and irrevocably, no ifs, ands, or buts."[39] If an *encomendero* no longer owns the slaves and lacks the financial means to acquire them back, he must be ready to *sell himself into slavery* to fulfill his commitment. At this point the prospective penitent, perhaps even the priest, must surely be asking himself whether such a bold program of reparation, even if embraced in the moment of confessional contrition, could really be adhered to when it comes time for such a massive divestiture of money and goods. To this end, Las Casas insists that the agreement of the penitent to all of these terms must be done through a public oath, "in legal and binding form," made in the presence of a notary or official of the government.[40] In fact, this insistence on legally binding plans of restitution is made repeatedly by Las Casas and is the most consistent theme of *Confesionario*. Expectations must be explained and affirmed, and all this before the penitent has even begun the actual confession!

During the sacrament itself "the confessor urges the penitent to have a deep, deep sorrow and regret for his enormous sins."[41] But not only his own sins: here comes Las Casas with yet another emphasis on the social nature of both sin and reparation:

> The penitent must regret not only what he committed with his own hands, he must be sorry as well for all the evils, all the harm done by those others he came out with. Each of them is responsible for the whole. The reasoning is this: every one of them who came out knew well why they came—to conquer, they all had exactly that purpose. . . . Each one is required to make restitution for what everyone stole, what everyone acquired so wickedly, for the damages

38. Casas, *De unico vocationis modo* 7, §5.

39. Casas, *Confesionario*, 283.

40. Ibid.

41. Ibid.

all did, even though a particular person did not gain or spend a cent of the fortune made.[42]

In this striking passage, Las Casas offers a challenging interpretation of shared moral agency. Later in the text, Las Casas even elevates to the category of *mortal sin* those involved in dealing weapons—"gunpowder, bullets, lances" that were then used in the violent oppression of Indians. He acknowledges that some of them did no actual violence themselves, but he is clear that their sin came in "the aid they give through the material of war," and thus "they are guilty of the whole thing."[43]

At points in *Confesionario*, Las Casas allows the priest some minor flexibility to mitigate the extent of reparation required, but, in general, a comprehensive plan is demanded. The reason for this marks, in my view, the most significant element in Las Casas' theory of reparation: penance links the salvation of individual sinners to the task of social reconstruction. And Las Casas takes into account not only the specific damage done by the individual but also the general needs of the affected community. For example, Las Casas instructs the priest to find out exactly who the penitent injured or exploited so that the victims may receive restitution. But then the text acknowledges a reality that complicates this task: "If there are no survivors, restitution shall be made for the good of their villages."[44] Moreover, he then considers the employment needed for this social reconstruction, and he recommends that Indians from nearby villages be allowed to join in, that they may receive "their livelihood, or sources of livelihood, or provisions to start them off."[45] One gets the sense that what Las Casas has in mind is a kind of "New Deal" series of social programs that are a reversal of the process of Conquest, an *undoing of its sins*. And in this program, Las Casas wants a personal encounter between *conquistadores* and Indians. To this end, "the penitent, personally, to the best of his ability, shall instruct them, look out for them, care for them, fend for and foster them, and, in sum, give them aid and comfort in their necessities."[46] It is in this aspect of personal encounter that, we will see, Las Casas comes closest to Aquinas' concept of satisfaction.

42. Ibid., 284.
43. Ibid., 288.
44. Ibid., 284.
45. Ibid.
46. Ibid., 286.

The emphasis on making clear the requirements of social repair to the penitent is so pronounced in *Confesionario* that, in fact, nowhere does it mention absolution. It is possible that after agreeing by oath to let the priest set the restitution, the penitent confesses and is given absolution immediately. This would square both with the strict demands for confession set by the Dominicans *and* the prevailing practice of the sacrament in his day. But the silence of the text does indicate at least some relativizing of the gift of God's forgiving grace within the process of reconciliation. Restitution is related to that process, but it alone cannot complete it. Las Casas himself had hinted at this earlier in his career, stating the need to go "beyond restitution to satisfaction." But what is striking in *Confesionario* is that he makes little distinction between the two terms. Usually he conflates them, though once he does suggest that some penitents, rather than being assigned a plan of restitution by the priest, may choose to "give it all back, make total satisfaction."[47] Here he captures the sense of wholeness in satisfaction, but still the text itself puts so much emphasis on the material dimension that it neglects the role of God's grace. In this way, Las Casas risked losing one of Aquinas' key insights.

Aquinas, Reparation, and the Satisfaction of Christ

In the first chapter, I defined penance as *the practices through which persons lament, take responsibility for, and seek to repair the wounds that are caused by sin.* As I have also argued, penance has both a natural and a theological dimension. I would like now to correlate restitution to the domain of natural practice and satisfaction to the domain of grace-enabled work. In this move, which I will root in Aquinas, I am not suggesting that restitution is fit for politics while satisfaction is fit only for the sacrament. To the contrary, by showing the essential but limited nature of restitution and the expansive and generative possibilities for satisfaction, I attempt to move beyond standard paradigms of social repair and into less familiar, but more innovative, strategies.

I propose a definition of restitution as *actions that return to a victim specific goods, whether items or rights or dominion, that were unjustly taken from them and that begin to restore a right relationship with the perpetrator and with society.* This definition emphasizes the return to the situation *ex ante* and the move *toward* restoration of right relationship. It also leaves

47. Ibid., 283.

space for the deepening of this essential work. Theologically, we can recall that, for Aquinas, restitution is an act of justice and that the human
practice of justice is necessary but not sufficient for salvation. Put another
way, in order to be perfected justice must be deepened through practices
that require grace. Thus, though I will develop Aquinas' account in more
detail below, I now will offer my own theological definition of satisfaction
as *the power by which God mercifully transforms persons from a life of sin
and injustice into a life of comprehensive right relationship with self, others,
creation, and God.* Satisfaction, I will note, is not conferred extrinsically,
but rather is experienced through participation in the repairing power of
Christ. In this sense, moral agency for reconciliation is not a competition
between human and divine action. God's work for justice does not begin
where our work leaves off, implying some division of labor of what both
parties can accomplish. Indeed, as my account of the New Testament in
chapter 1 argued, the ministry of reconciliation is the work of the Holy
Spirit in us *and through us.* Moreover, as the work of the Spirit, the power
of satisfaction is not limited to ecclesial practices. Yet, before I explore the
possibilities for broad application, I first must treat the theological contours
of satisfaction, and to do that I will turn directly to Aquinas.

The Dominican Romanus Cessario emphasizes that, for Aquinas, satisfaction is comprehensive atonement through the saving life, death, and
resurrection of Christ.[48] That is, Christ atones for the sins of the world because, suffering through our injustices, he reveals and becomes the way to
justice, life, and our ultimate common good: God. In an interesting phrase,
Aquinas himself describes humanity not only as *imago Dei* but also *ad
imaginem*, toward the image of God, "by which is signified a certain movement toward perfection."[49] Satisfaction is the completion of this movement
and thus, obviously, only Christ has attained it, though as our brother and
savior, the "first born of all creation," he opens the way and is the way for us.

Aquinas himself defines satisfaction in a way that begins to show the
several layers of his approach:

> A man effectively satisfies for an offense when he offers to the one
> who has been offended something which he accepts as matching
> or outweighing the former offense. . . . Christ, suffering in a lov-
> ing and obedient spirit, offered more to God than was demanded
> in recompense for all the sins of mankind because, first, the love

48. See Cessario, *Christian Satisfaction*, 152.

49. ST I 35.2 ad 3.

which led him to suffer was a great love; second, the life he laid down in satisfaction was of great dignity, since it was the life of God and of man; and third, his suffering was all-embracing and his pain so great. Christ's passion, then, was not only sufficient but superabundant satisfaction for the sins of mankind.[50]

Though he begins here with a concept that looks like the justice of restitution—matching the offense—he moves deeper toward the satisfaction of love, which ultimately generates an "all-embracing" solidarity. The justice displayed by Christ is thus not contained by the calculation of due—Christ was sinless, after all, and did not "owe" restitution—but is transformed into a sacrificial gift. And in Christ, satisfaction is ultimately not a one-to-one balance, since he "offered more" than what was needed, overpowering sin by "superabundance." Aquinas also makes clear that satisfaction is completed in Christ not for the sake of "appeasing" God. God is already whole and holy, but satisfaction makes possible *for us* a wholeness that other practices, even restitution, cannot achieve. Cessario thus emphasizes that Christ's action re-establishes right relationship. As he puts it, "The work of satisfaction *is* the work of reconciliation," and the love-infused justice revealed in Christ is "decidedly interpersonal."[51]

In this sense, the sacrifice of Jesus can be seen in light of a divine pedagogy on display for us to see, learn, and practice. In arguing that the Passion was not the only conceivable way of "healing our misery" but, given the human condition, the only "suitable" one, Aquinas notes that Christ makes whole, satisfies, our ultimate end as persons because, in seeing the love of God for us, we are "stirred to love him" in return through "the example . . . of justice and the other virtues displayed in the Passion, which are requisite for man's salvation."[52] Elsewhere he says that Christ's actions "excite our charity."[53] Aquinas is not suggesting that Christ's value is merely instructive; it is that, but the incarnation of God also changes the moral structure of the universe and opens truly new possibilities for our participation in the divine-human relationship. Indeed, nothing in this paradigm suggests that we stand idly by while a "magic wand" of salvation moves us from the debit to credit column. Rather, Aquinas goes on to argue clearly that it is by being incorporated into the body of Christ, "as members are into the head,"

---

50. ST III 48.2.

51. Cessario, *Christian Satisfaction*, 143, 214.

52. ST III 46.3

53. ST III 49.1

that we can share in his satisfaction.[54] And that means work. The victorious act has been performed, but "in order to secure [its] effects, we must be likened unto him."[55] This comes, of course, through baptism and the life of the church. And when, after baptism, we sin, we too must undertake the work of satisfaction to repair relationships we have ruptured, though Aquinas argues that our job is made lighter "by the co-operation of Christ's satisfaction."[56] The dynamic interchange between our tasks of repairing sin in our own lives and the saving reparation of Christ for the world brings us to the place where that divine co-operation is most evident for Aquinas— the sacrament of penance.

Satisfaction and the Sacrament of Penance

Perhaps the best way to understand the finality of Christ's cure for sin and the ongoing need for treatment is to construe satisfaction as medicinal power. Indeed, not unlike the Irish monks, Aquinas construes the sacrament of penance in just this way. Eric Luijten explains that, for Aquinas, the medicine does not work mechanically—"like a pill," which would construe sacraments as things that "do the trick"—but rather relationally, gathering the church around "the physician of our souls," who himself is the doctor and the medicine who heals us.[57] Aquinas observes that God can heal completely and all at once, but also "little by little."[58] Indeed, baptism, for Aquinas, is an all-at-once healing in which incorporation into Christ's body is satisfactory precisely because of Christ, since we contribute no satisfaction in this sacrament. But, after this, when we freely choose the disorder of sin, then the medicine of the sacrament of penance is necessary *for our sake* to be reconfigured to Christ and freely choose to participate in his satisfaction "according to the measure of [our] personal acts."[59] For this reason, namely, the ongoing need for personal conversion in our lives, Aquinas describes the sacrament of penance as "a spiritual medicine, which can frequently be repeated."[60]

54. ST III 49.3 ad 3.

55 Ibid., ad 2.

56. Ibid.

57. Luijten, *Sacramental Forgiveness*, 54–55.

58. ST III 86.5 ad 1.

59. Ibid., III 86.4 ad 3.

60. Ibid., III 84.10 ad 5.

In the practice of the sacrament, Aquinas defines the key actions of the penitent as contrition, confession, and satisfaction.[61] Satisfaction here refers to the penances given by the priest by which the penitent participates in the reconciling power of Christ. The distinction with restitution—which is *not* the name of the final element of the sacrament—is worth revisiting. As we saw, Las Casas recognized that some sins require going "beyond restitution to satisfaction" and sacramental healing. But his practice as described in *Confesionario* never actually followed Aquinas' thick, and hopeful, account of the way in which a penitent's acts of satisfaction participate in the definitive satisfaction of Christ. So in what *precise* ways do acts of satisfaction "go beyond" restitution for Aquinas? We cannot say. My answer to this question may seem the ultimate dodge, but I blame Aquinas! As I noted, he stopped writing the *Summa* mid-treatment of penance. More precisely, he was on the cusp of taking up just this question when he had his inconvenient moment with the Lord. Fortunately, he had addressed the topic earlier in his career, in the *Commentary on the Sentences of Peter Lombard*, and this engagement is thus the best approximation of his view.[62]

Lombard had argued that what marks an act of satisfaction is that it "cures past sins and preserves against future ones."[63] Aquinas agrees, since the acts of satisfaction imposed by the priest are intended to be a holistically restorative punishment. But a dispute arose as to whether restitution is properly a part of that satisfaction. Lombard argued yes, using the dictum of Augustine that "a sin is not removed unless restitution is made."[64] While Aquinas agreed with Augustine's dictum, he did not agree with Lombard that restitution is a part of satisfaction. Aquinas begins by clarifying that restitution is actually not what the priest prescribes in the sacrament. Rather, the matter that comes under the *arbitrio sacerdotis*, judgment of the priest, is that which establishes reconciliation: satisfaction. In parsing the distinction, Aquinas comes close to proposing the dichotomy that restitution concerns our relationship to neighbors while satisfaction concerns our relationship to God, but he stops short of this. The real driving element

---

61. Ibid., III 90.1-4.

62. A further inconvenience arises in that this section of the *Commentary* has not been translated into English, and thus I am relying largely on my own translations. Still, I believe that my limited insights can help point the way to fresh research on this topic in Aquinas. I am indebted to theologian Annie McGowan, who helped me with the translation as she worked from the French text and I from the Latin.

63. Lombard, in Luijten, *Sacramental Forgiveness*, 155

64. See Brett, *Liberty, Right and Nature*, 23.

of the distinction for him is that restitution is directed toward *material* compensation and satisfaction toward the *moral and spiritual* reform of relationships.

One way of stating this distinction is to say that restitution seeks justice and satisfaction seeks love. Consider my translation of his most detailed passage from the *Commentary*:

> Reparation of inequality in things is restitution; satisfaction applies to reparation of inequalities in actions and passions. Sometimes there is satisfaction without any restitution, as when someone humbles himself before the neighbor about whom he has spoken hateful words. Sometimes there is restitution without satisfaction, as when someone returns an item that belongs to another. Sometimes both are required, as when someone takes something from another through violence, which offends both the neighbor and God. Some thus say that the restitution [in this case] is not part of satisfaction, since it is not due only to God and is not part of the judgment of the priest, but [I say] rather that this restitution is a preamble to satisfaction.[65]

dsHere we can see Aquinas articulate a view that the restitution due to our harmed neighbors is required for but not proper to the sacrament. While he disagrees with a portion of the reasoning referenced in "some thus say . . . ," he affirms that restitution is "preambulum ad satisfactionem," a preamble to satisfaction. This striking phrase—later invoked two more times by Aquinas—is evocative of precisely what Las Casas recommended by requiring oaths to do reparation *before* entering the sacrament. One could even argue that Aquinas' idea here goes further, suggesting that ideally the work of restitution should be *completed* before, preambular to, the sacramental encounter that offers God's grace to deepen the reparation with satisfactory acts.

But Aquinas is not really making here, or anywhere, a "sequential" argument about finishing the one before starting the other. His nature-grace paradigm is not so much two tiers, the latter on top of the former, as it is a perfecting penetration of grace that transforms natural virtues like justice and enables supernatural virtues like love. In this way, the sacramental grace of penance can propel the work of restitution, but this happens precisely because of participation in the satisfactory work of Christ. That is, what *marks* the sacraments is the power of satisfaction, unleashed in the

---

65. Aquinas, *Scriptum super libros Sententiarum*, IV.15.1.5, at 159–60.

encounter with the priest and also in acts directed toward God and victims. So Aquinas is not setting up a rigid sequence, since the two categories of acts are performed by the same penitent on the same journey to reconciliation. I would even propose that the use of the term "preambulum" need not suggest *before* in the temporal sense. Since *ambulare* refers primarily to the act of walking, Aquinas may be suggesting that the need for restitution is always *in front of* the penitent on the journey toward reconciliation. I could even stretch the metaphor and suggest that walking before the penitent is Christ, who is ahead of us on the journey as the embodiment of a restitution so deep that it has become satisfaction.

In any case, when Aquinas argues that the priest properly assigns acts of satisfaction *and not restitution*, he is not denying the necessity of justice. Aquinas assumes a political system of justice that deals with restitution in cases of serious wrong, thus working in tandem with the sacrament. Such a system was sorely lacking, of course, after the Conquest, and so we can be sympathetic to Las Casas' insistence that the priest assign restitution. And nothing in Aquinas' treatment would discourage a priest from making clear that the demands of justice cannot be sacrificed as the acts of penance are done. My point here, though, is not to suggest a particular model of the sacrament. Rather I wish to highlight that Aquinas emphasizes the need for a practice that has a deeper aim than restitution, one focused on transforming "actions and passions." That practice is satisfaction.

We can now return for a moment to the text above where Aquinas ends by saying "some thus say" that acts of restitution made to the harmed neighbor cannot be satisfaction *because* they are not directed solely to God. He agrees that such acts are not satisfaction, but he quickly rejects the rationale by pointing out that "this will not hold, since every sin committed against a neighbor is committed against God. Love of neighbor is included in love of God. Thus satisfaction to God is associated with satisfaction to neighbor."[66] As the text develops, Aquinas begins to reveal the real reason why restitution made to the neighbor is not part of satisfaction. Consider, he says, one who has made restitution to a neighbor and stops harming them: "If all he does is stop sinning, or cease to offend, he has not found reconciliation for the offense. . . . This in no way is part of satisfaction, but rather a preamble."[67] Thus Aquinas argues that "we should well concede that satisfaction done toward the neighbor is part of the satisfaction

66. Ibid., at 161.
67. Ibid., at 163.

rendered to God, but restitution is not part of this satisfaction made to neighbor or to God."[68] Admittedly, Aquinas' point here places him in some tension with the earlier tradition—not only Lombard but the Irish monks, who tended to construe acts of restoring material goods as acts of satisfaction. But Aquinas guards the difference. And I would propose that he is making a significant move in two respects.

First, Aquinas preserves the demands of justice on their own merits. Restitution can never be dispensed—not even by the priest in the sacrament—and it thus also cannot be spiritualized in a way that ignores the material claims of victims.[69] Indeed, one critique of contemporary efforts in truth and reconciliation is that they move too quickly toward an idealized restoration of relationship when in fact inequalities and imbalances that were the context for the harm remain. Aquinas offers a corrective to this. His insistence that restitution is a preamble to satisfaction guards against minimizing the justice due to victims. Second, by noting what restitution cannot do, Aquinas clears a space for what he sees as the necessary deepening of justice into the more transformative action of love. But sinners need to be capacitated for this new life of love. Even after restitution is made, contrition felt, confession spoken, and absolution given, the residue of disorder—ever threatening to bring forth injustice again—remains. Acts of satisfaction, through which the penitent co-operates with grace, repair this underlying disorder and are directed toward a new and deeper life with God and neighbors.

While it is in his *Commentary on the Sentences* that Aquinas explicitly distinguishes restitution and satisfaction, his insights are also on display in the *Summa*. For example, in the final question of the *Summa* before he stopped writing, Aquinas introduces the parts of penance and argues that satisfaction seeks "not only the restoration of the equality of justice" but "also and still more the reconciliation of friendship, which is accomplished by the offender making atonement according to the will of the person offended."[70] This is a remarkable passage because we do see a development in his thought. As before, the justice of restitution does not "fall away" but rather is deepened into a vision of friendship between perpetrator and victim. But here, Aquinas is explicit that the terms of that friendship are made *according to the will of the victim*. The reparation of the penitent, in a sense,

68. Ibid., at 164.

69. See ibid., at 151 and 159–60.

70. ST III 90.2.

must be guided by the will of the victim. Indeed, in this same passage, he notes the inadequacy of the justice "of judges" for whom "the discretion of the offender or of the person offended" is not taken into account.[71] This inadequacy, as we will see, is known all too well to victims still seeking reparation in the wake of official truth and reconciliation processes.

The Political Relevance of Satisfaction

In 2005, the United Nations General Assembly published "basic principles and guidelines" for the implementation of reparations for victims of gross violations of human rights. In the text, the UN identifies four dimensions of reparation. The first three are restitution, compensation, and rehabilitation for victims, which are aimed at returning them to their situation *ex ante*, but the fourth and final element is "satisfaction." This term, given its thoroughgoing theological provenance, is quite surprising. For the UN text, satisfaction is what ensures non-repetition of the injustice and guarantees all of those acts aimed at "restoring the dignity, the reputation and the rights of the victim and of persons closely connected with the victim."[72] This is to include public disclosure of the wrongs; acts of official apology and commemorations, including the reburial of located human remains; punishment of perpetrators; and education for the community "at all levels" to ensure that the injustice is not repeated.[73] It would require another book to locate in the linguistic and judicial history the precise migration of the theological concept of satisfaction to the political notion employed by the UN. I would note briefly that among the UN's four practices of reparation, satisfaction is by far the most comprehensive and holistic. In fact, the text goes on to endorse legal remedies and expansive mechanisms "for preventing and monitoring social conflicts and their resolution."[74] Moreover, Max du Plessis identifies satisfaction as the domain that treats the moral dimension of political injustice.[75] While the UN does not appeal to the universal jurisdiction of God, it does recognize that satisfaction must employ the most powerful means at a society's disposal, not only to repair the wounds of victims but to establish the comprehensive justice of right relationship.

71. Ibid.

72. United Nations General Assembly, *Basic Principles*, 22.

73. Ibid.

74. Ibid., 23.

75. See Du Plessis, "Reparations and International Law," 41–69.

I suggest that the use of the term *satisfaction* in the UN text points to the promise of developing the political application of this concept. Indeed, even the word *satisfaction* itself has a kind of cross-boundary appeal in both theological and secular discourse. As the UN text shows, the goal of satisfaction appeals to the desire for wholeness on the part of victims and broken societies, a wholeness that is more than compensatory. Working to holistically repair our wounds is a universal trait of human nature, and thus the language employed by the UN does not appear forced or extrinsic to the kinds of conversations that happen in the wake of injustice. Indeed, the only audience for whom the word *satisfaction* strikes a dissonant chord is those of us who know its theological history. Still, it must be admitted that the use of the word has a kind of generality and vagueness about its meaning and measure in approaches to reparation. And thus I hope to use the theological roots of the concept to flesh out what acts of satisfaction might look like in the political arena—and how those acts differ from the current practices on offer to societies seeking reconciliation.

The basic lesson, gleaned from Aquinas and evident in the UN text, is this: in pursuit of reparation, we often fail not by seeking too much but by seeking too little. Put another way, when we reduce reparation to restitution, we withdraw an important horizon of possibility for new relationship. The lack of this horizon of hope tends to focus on the past and present predicament, giving no resources to stoke hearts and imaginations toward a fresh future. In this confined context, perpetrators will either refuse to engage personally in the work of reparation or will do the minimum in order to achieve their goal—be it absolution or amnesty. But in the Thomistic paradigm, such goals are not rewards but rather gifts that allow perpetrators to *experience* the kind of action appropriate for their victims. In situations of deep social injustice, to affirm the need for a horizon of hope in victims but not in perpetrators is appealing but, ultimately, wrong. It is wrong not only because it runs against the purposes of God, from whom mercy comes without merit, but also because it is counterproductive to the practical goal of social repair, which often requires the support of perpetrators to become a reality.

For Aquinas, of course, the sacrament of penance is the primary means by which God *capacitates* penitents for such work. The power at work in the sacrament is itself relevant for social repair, but it also has implications for a wide range of other political practices. As I noted in chapter 1, Aquinas teaches us that while sacraments are the ordinary means of grace, we must also remember that "Deus non alligatur sacramentis"—God is not bound to the sacraments.[76] This does not mean to cast our view away from a sacrament like penance but rather to look deeply into it for glimpses of how God, who created the whole universe, intends human beings to flourish.

Penance, as we have seen, is the only sacrament that Aquinas also treats as a *virtue*.[77] I want now to close this chapter by suggesting practical ways that this virtue can help societies create horizons of new hope as they pursue truth and reconciliation projects. First, the virtue of penance challenges the standard construal of reparations as material transfers of money, goods, and services.[78] Reparations specialist Pablo de Greiff recounts an interesting story from Peru in this regard. As the work of the Truth and Reconciliation Commission there was engaged in its process of hearings and meetings to establish recommendations for going forward, the Inter-American Court of Human Rights issued to plaintiffs major financial awards that, if broadened to all victims, would have exceeded the national budget of the country.[79] De Greiff reports that these court rulings may well have contributed to the overall resistance to reparations. He does not suggest, nor would I, that these rulings were unjust or that the judicial system should stay out of reparations paradigms. Indeed, as I have noted, the law is a significant teacher in the cultivation of virtue, especially justice. But Aquinas reminds us that as a virtue, penance requires a broader horizon beyond restitution in order to take hold. And, if the virtue does not take hold, then even the restitutive aspect of penance is in jeopardy—a case of which Peru is a classic example. What is needed in addition to legal judgments are acts of satisfaction, by which perpetrators can see themselves as agents of change and through which a more stable and consistent virtue can be generated. If we can recover this key insight, once neglected on this continent after the Conquest, Aquinas' work might finally represent a fruitful "*Summa* for the Americas," ripe for redeployment in Peru.

Are there examples elsewhere of satisfaction actually working, coming not at the expense of material restitution but rather promoting the holistic virtue of penitential justice? I would present the case of post-Holocaust Germany as an example of success. To date, $70 billion has been paid in material compensation for Nazi crimes, and this restitution has been

76. ST III 68.2.

77. ST III.84.1,7 and III.85.3. See Morrow, "Reconnecting Sacrament and Virtue," 304–20.

78. See Philpott, *Just and Unjust Peace*, 191.

79. De Greiff, *Handbook of Reparations*, 456–57.

supported by a constellation of practices aimed at generating a new horizon. Through common projects such as revising textbooks, learning about victims, and engaging in public discussion, Germany was able to build a "culture of contrition" and inculcate the virtue of penance.[80] An embodiment of that virtue came when West German Chancellor Willy Brandt dropped to his knees in sorrow at a Warsaw memorial in 1970. Philpott names such acts as acknowledgment and apology, key elements in his ethic of reconciliation. For my purposes, I would emphasize the way in which such practices generate a new horizon of hope and possibility and thus qualify as acts of satisfaction that promote the virtue of penance. While Germany has not been without obstacles on the road to repair, the figure of $70 billion at least shows that restitution need not be sacrificed in pursuing a robust penitential ethic. On the contrary, acts of satisfaction can be quite practical in helping drive the process by which the demands of justice penetrate more deeply into the habits of a society.

Another example of a society that has tried, though with even more mixed results, to incorporate the virtue of penance is Guatemala. In the wake of almost four decades of civil war and military impunity for political deaths and disappearances, the Catholic Church launched the Recovery of Historical Memory Project (REMHI). Eight hundred trained "agents of reconciliation" were deployed throughout the country, even to the remotest villages where many Mayans had been killed.[81] In Spanish, these agents were called "animadores" (animators), and their job was to promote the kinds of practices invoked in my definition of penance—especially the lament that properly follows injustice. REMHI did not attempt to adjudicate claims of material restitution but to educate the country as a whole on the human face behind those claims. And REMHI explicitly offered a new horizon in which to see a way forward. Through local-level workshops, Guatemalans were given tools for reconciling perpetrators and victim-survivors, who might often live within the same community. The ambitious project sought by REMHI was not fully realized, in part because of the assassination of its leader, Bishop Juan Gerardi. Killed two days after the release of REMHI's report in April 1998, Gerardi is a kind of martyr for the virtue of penance. And REMHI provides us with a concrete and extensive example of the recognition that the deep work of conversion is necessary to capacitate a society for the work of reparation.

80. See Philpott, *Just and Unjust Peace*, 199.

81. See ibid., 186.

We might also imagine the ways in which the use of "animators" might be applied not just to the community of victims but to perpetrators as well. What if teams were deployed with the purpose of engaging in personal encounters with alleged perpetrators? Such agents of reconciliation need not be officials of a court or government—perhaps they would be sponsored by church and civic groups—and certainly they would often be rebuffed. Still, even the smallest progress in offering to perpetrators the experience of a new way forward would be of tremendous value. It might also divert the usual post-conflict process by which implicated individuals are routed into patterns of denial and dismissal. Of course, sometimes these people *are* innocent, but when a large swath of a society refuses to acknowledge mass crime, we can recognize a vice at work—to which the response should be the inculcation of virtue. Attention to animating a turn toward the virtue of penance is thus worth exploration. The goal can be pursued in myriad ways. In Rwanda, "gacaca courts" brought victims and perpetrators together on village hillsides in the presence of a community exerting social pressure in favor of penitence. This brought some problems—insincere confessions and forced forgiveness among them—but it also led to creative penances tied to social repair. Rather than languishing in prison, former killers were able to work off some of their punishment on behalf of victim-survivors. Such acts of manual labor and personal service promote the "humbling of one's self" that Aquinas saw as a trademark of satisfaction. No doubt, the examples I have mentioned from Germany, Guatemala, and Rwanda are immersed in complex dynamics of promise and dysfunction, as is the case of Peru, to which I will turn in great detail in chapter 6. I am not offering here facile means to solve these dilemma of reconciliation but only trying to stoke the political imagination to consider other alternatives to construing and reaching that goal.

The moral philosopher Margaret Urban Walker argues that a dimension of justice too often ignored in the civil arena is hope.[82] Paradigms that are articulated solely in reference to past wrongs and material compensation will fail to exemplify a new possibility for the society and fail to construct a basis for trust among the people. In this way, for Walker as well as for Philpott, reparations ought to be expressive, communicating solidarity and signaling a fresh way forward for social justice. Walker even turns to the *Summa* to articulate the way in which hope must be paramount as reparations are sought: what is needed is deep and sustained attention to

82. See Walker, *Moral Repair*, 40–44.

what Aquinas called the "raising of the spirits toward the realization of the arduous good."[83] Indeed, this is the crux of the way in which the penitential ethic I propose is shaped by the influence of Aquinas. The case for a specific program of reparations is never an abstract matter but must always account for the need to generate a capacity to sustain that program among the people, and particularly among those who routinely obstruct its progress. In light of that perennial obstacle, I am thus suggesting that political communities would do well to explicitly cultivate the virtue of penance—and the acts of satisfaction that embody it. No doubt, this suggestion is full of challenges, but it can also contribute to that most fundamental need after situations of deep injustice: the "raising of the spirits toward the realization of the arduous good."

83. ST I-II 25.1. See Walker, *What Is Reparative Justice?*, 46.

4

The Penitential Pope:
John Paul II and the Jubilee

SPEAKING TO CLOSE THE 1983 Synod of Bishops, which focused on penance and reconciliation in the mission of the church, Pope John Paul II issued a remarkable challenge. His call goes to the heart of my proposal for an ethic of social repair rooted in Catholic penitential tradition and ordered toward the complex problems facing the human community:

> If one may and must speak in an analogical sense about social sin, and also about structural sin—since sin is properly an act of the person—for us, as pastors and theologians, the following problem arises: which penance and which reconciliation must correspond to this analogical sin?[1]

The pope's immediate context was the need to reform and rejuvenate the sacrament of penance, which was under intense scrutiny and revision during the Synod. Indeed, a myriad of proposals had surfaced about confessional practice. The Bishops of Ghana had recommended fuller use of "general absolution"—in which the priestly word of forgiveness is pronounced to a group rather than an individual—to correspond to "African realities." They also proposed the use of communal "days of penance" in their dioceses.[2] Cardinal Bernardin of Chicago suggested an optional new rite—with echoes of the Irish model—that would place a shared journey of penance, guided by a spiritual director for a group in a parish setting, between the time of individual confession to a priest and a return for

---

1. John Paul II, "Value of This Collegial Body," 65.
2. Lodonu, "Reconciliation and African Realities," 350.

absolution (individual or general) within a communal liturgy.[3] Ultimately, the pope ratified the status quo of sacramental practice, allowing general absolution only in extraordinary cases. In doing so, he affirmed the view of Cardinal Ratzinger at the Synod: "Sacraments must be personally received . . . given to a specific person and not to the group."[4]

Debates over the confessional are important, but the challenge issued by John Paul during the Synod to explore new forms of penance—forms that correspond to social and structural sin—is not limited to sacramental practice. His provocative call deserves a fuller exploration of possibilities in the realm of politics. And no call was more provocative than his Jubilee Year campaign to lament, take responsibility for, and seek to repair the sins in which the church has historically been implicated. This campaign was part of his larger penitential commitment: Vatican reporter Luigi Accattoli counted more than one hundred ecclesial *mea culpas* issued by John Paul II. To be sure, not all of these apologies led to wider programs of penance. The most notable failure has been evident in responses to the sexual abuse crisis, which I will examine later in the chapter. Still, the events leading up to and following the special "Day of Pardon" liturgy at St. Peter's Basilica on the first Sunday of Lent in 2000 provide a fruitful opportunity to explore the broader call of John Paul to social forms of reconciliation. Thus, his Jubilee actions will be the subject of this chapter as I explore the ways that the pope provided resources to reimagine the public dimension of penitential acts.

Setting the Stage: Awareness of Sin's Social Nature

Before analyzing John Paul's provocative gestures, it is important to note that he was not original in promoting an understanding of the social nature of sin. In this section, I will trace the rise of this understanding in Catholic theology. In fact, the Council of Trent, which concluded in 1563 and is often associated with an individualistic model, set in motion the developments that enabled John Paul to speak of concepts like "structures of sin." In particular, as I noted in chapter 1, the Council insisted that "absolution takes away sin, but it does not remedy all the disorders sin has caused." And the 1566 Tridentine Catechism ascribed to the confessor a social role as "the good pastor binding the wounds of his sheep and healing them with

---

3. Bernardin, "New Rite of Penance," 324–26.
4. Ratzinger, "Necessity of Personal Confession," 331.

the medicine of penance."[5] Moreover, Trent called for the establishment of seminaries to explore "what appears useful for the hearing of confessions."[6] The most famous of these seminaries was the Jesuit-run Roman College (now called the Pontifical Gregorian University), which became the site for the rise of *casuistry*, a methodology that deserves special mention in the history of penance as a form of social repair.

James Keenan, SJ and Thomas Shannon locate the rise of casuistry in a seventeenth-century form of globalization in which "age-old moral rules were unable to entertain the new and unfamiliar circumstances" of interconnected systems of commerce and politics.[7] As a result, they departed from a deductive approach and, instead, tried to create a system from the bottom up, working with *cases*—thus the term *casuistry*. No doubt, the endless variations of details and circumstances at work in particular cases would allow for the acceptance of "probable" conclusions that exempted the penitent from a seemingly stable moral norm. General prohibitions, ranging from usury to murder, were re-examined in light of cases to give individuals more latitude for action. Casuist defenders argued that their goal was to shift the focus away from morality as individual culpability in order to illuminate social dynamics and communal responsibility for sin, but critics, such as Blaise Pascal, saw the concessions as "false rules" that allow for just about everything except "sinning just for the sake of sinning."[8] As a result, the challenge was (and is) to develop a paradigm sensitive to social circumstance but insistent on responsibility for sin.

St. Alphonsus Liguori tried to meet that challenge. Writing in the mid-1700s, Liguori became known for proposing a kind of middle ground between the model of priest as judge and the Casuist inclination toward priest as defense attorney. Appreciation for distinct cases and mitigating circumstances is evident in Liguori's writing, but for him, the purpose of moral theology is not to find loopholes. The goal, rather, is growth in holiness. The word most often attributed to his style is *pastoral*: penitents need the experience of a shepherd—or as he himself put it, "a father, full of charity."[9] In one sense, his approach to confessions did minimize the scope of restitutive justice, a trend still evident today. For example, in cases in

---

5. *Catechism of the Council of Trent*, 2.5.1, in Mahoney, *Making of Moral Theology*, 24.

6. Ibid.

7. Keenan and Shannon, *Context of Casuistry*, xvi.

8. Ibid.

9. Liguori, *Selected Writings*, 317.

which "rough-mannered people will not be persuaded to give back," the confessor should prescribe restitution "without explaining the amount, letting each person make restitution as conscience dictates."[10] He also allows for a penitent who cannot identify a victim to have Masses said as restitution, and, for poor penitents, "restitution can be applied in favor of himself or his family."[11] Liguori even counsels that a priest should omit a warning about restitution if he is certain it would go unheeded, since "a material sin should not be made into a formal sin."[12] In these examples, Liguori seems to be a penitential minimalist.

On the other hand, Liguori here is offering a way forward for the precise kinds of cases in which the more severe approach (which we saw on display in the last chapter with Las Casas) often fails to break through. A consistent theme of his writings is desire that confession not "frighten people" such that they do not return. Rather, he wants sinners to experience "an open-hearted welcome" that can grow into "a sense of joy" in penitents and confessors at "the good fortune of having snatched a soul from the hands of the evil one."[13] Liguori here recognizes the need of sinners to experience the tenderness of God that then generates their own fresh revival in moving toward a new horizon of justice and love. Thus, like Aquinas, he is a constructive resource in the search for a penitential ethic capable of responding creatively to the deep wounds of social injustice. But I also propose that he helps develop the need for a *communal* element in penance, an element that grows in the twentieth century and is exemplified in John Paul II. Specifically, he advances categories of cooperation with evil to understand more fully how people can be responsible for sins they did not directly commit.

In his classic *Theologia Moralis*, Liguori makes his fullest statement on the levels of cooperation with evil:

> That [cooperation] is *formal* which concurs in the bad will of the [principal agent], and it cannot be without sin. That [cooperation] is *material* which concurs only in the bad action of the [principal agent], apart from the cooperator's intention. The latter [material cooperation] is licit when the action is good or indifferent in itself, and when one has a reason for doing it that is both just and

10. Ibid., 321
11. Ibid.
12. Ibid.
13. Ibid., 317

proportioned to the gravity of the [principal agent's] sin and to the closeness of the assistance which is given to the carrying out of that sin.[14]

Since formal cooperation is always wrong, the focus for Liguori is how to determine when material cooperation can be justified. Catholic tradition has maintained that *immediate* material cooperation is also always wrong. This occurs when a cooperator foresees (though does not intend) an evil and still provides essential, material assistance in the commission of the sin. At the other extreme, *remote* material cooperation refers to the common occurrence when we do have a small role in bad acts being committed, but we neither intend nor even foresee them, and our role is not essential. And, thus, there is no sin. In between is the category of *proximate* material cooperation with evil. Here the cooperator is substantively, though not essentially, contributing to the material conditions necessary for the sin. For Liguori, a good reason—unconnected to the rationale of the bad act—can permit such cooperation as long as it is "proportioned to the gravity" of the offense, meaning that the more we foresee our facilitation of a bad act, and the more evil that act seems, the better reason we must have for our own action. Two final elements can be briefly stated: the potential to give *scandal* (by creating wrong impressions about morality) raises the bar for cooperation, and situations of *duress* (pressure on one's life or livelihood) mitigate culpability.

I have briefly sketched these categories not in order to pinpoint precisely a system that Liguori invented. Concepts of cooperation existed before him and have gone well beyond what he specifically wrote. But he did pioneer a trend to examine the terrain beyond direct, formal responsibility for sin. Not only did his approach gain ecclesiastical approval—he was proclaimed patron saint of confessors and moral theologians—but it paved the way for increased awareness of the social dynamics of sin. This awareness, as Margaret Pfeil notes, comes to be robustly displayed in the pontificate of John Paul II, who advanced concepts of sin and repair that were deeply social.[15]

I have identified the role of Liguori in this trajectory, but others deserve mention too. In exploring early modern Catholic social thought, Michael Schuck argues that figures like Frédéric Ozanam, who began the Society of St. Vincent de Paul, and Bishop Wilhelm von Ketteler, whose

---

14. Liguori, *Theologia Moralis*, II, §63.

15. See Pfeil, "Toward an Understanding of the Language of Social Sin."

"organological approach" saw associations—not individuals—as the key moral agents, helped advance a social analysis of sin and its repair.[16] Moreover, Schuck catalogs nineteenth-century movements *outside of the church* that laid the indispensable foundation for John Paul's synthesis of sin and social analysis. To a world hurtling headlong into industrial capitalism, Karl Marx pointed out the scope of *commodification*—an insight theologians would use to describe "structures of sin." In a world ever more empirical and scientific, Max Weber noted the rise of *rationalization*, an antidote to which would be a penitential ethic rooted not in precise calculations of guilt but in a shared "solidarity of sin." And Emile Durkheim brought the problem of *specialization* to nineteenth-century consciousness so that later thinkers—including John Paul II—might resist the tendency to relegate the church's competence in repairing sin to matters of "private morality."[17] In these ways, as Schuck so helpfully demonstrates, the century preceding the rise of "Catholic Social Teaching" actually tilled the soil from which concepts of socially embedded sin emerged. And while Christians in every age have been aware of the ways in which sin and penance are always public matters, the church at the dawn of the twentieth century encountered massively complex systems of injustice that were global, impersonal, and aggressive.

As Pfeil depicts in detail, the Catholic vision of reconciliation grew in the twentieth century to respond to these corrosive social forces by issuing a call to personal conversion *and* structural transformation. Pope Leo XIII initiates this shift in stance by bringing to the level of encyclical the "social question" plaguing the industrial world and causing misery for most of its workers. While *Rerum novarum* did not engage in structural analysis—and is even skeptical of systems that promise relief of ills that arise from original sin and "are with man as long as life lasts"—Leo does demand that "some remedy must be found, and found quickly" for the plight of the poor.[18] In the text, Leo calls for legal safeguards for workers' pay and conditions, for a restraint on greed among owners, and for "harmony and agreement among social classes."[19] What is most relevant here to the future witness of popes like John Paul II is that Leo seeks to place the church squarely in the struggle for social repair. Previously, even amid the revolutions of the 1800s, popes

16. Schuck, "Early Modern Roman Catholic Social Thought," 99–124.

17. Ibid., 118.

18. Leo XIII, *Rerum novarum*, 2, 14.

19. Ibid., 15.

had attempted to shield the church from such struggles. But Leo, as Pfeil observes, set a precedent by using his most public platform to make clear "an awareness of the social dimensions of sin and an ecclesial commitment to address them."[20] Indeed, Leo also helps make the case for the precise role of religion—with its penitential and sacrificial approach—in pursuing social repair. He argues that "the church has a power peculiar to itself" and locates this power in the virtue of love, which alone "can destroy the evil at its root."[21] As we will see, John Paul's expansive notion of penance makes this same move: the burden of social sin is not cast off as the fault of others, but rather it is brought into the realm of ecclesial and personal responsibility.

Pope Benedict XV continued to focus on social repair, facing this task before, during, and after the First World War. In this way, his insight is relevant to the ethic I will propose for helping soldiers bear the burdens of conflict. Benedict was called the "peace pope" because he opposed all sides in the war. Interestingly, his efforts to dissuade U.S. entrance were rebuffed by Cardinal James Gibbons of Baltimore, leader of American Catholicism, who, in a letter to President Wilson, vowed that "our people, as ever, will rise as one man to serve the nation" in the call to war "with the holy sentiments of truest patriotic fervor."[22] After the carnage, Pope Benedict called for reconciliation, with particular attention to those "who carry on their bodies the ravages of this atrocious war."[23] Unless the peace penetrates to this personal level, he argued, all of the governmental treaties and accords simply will not last. Moreover, the pope warned, if the terms of reconciliation are punitive and omit the need for forgiveness, then "the germs of former enmities remain" and will re-emerge in more conflict.[24] This observation, of course, was prescient: reparations saddled Germany with a heavy burden, and the world again erupted in conflict a generation later. For purposes of a postwar ethic, we can note that while Benedict cautions that forgiveness and reconciliation must not violate "the rights of justice"—offending parties should be held to account—he also resists a strict accounting mechanism to parse out guilt among nations. Rather, he is convinced that not only individuals but *entire peoples* can engage in efforts

---

20. Pfeil, "Toward an Understanding," 38.

21. *Rerum novarum*, 22, 45.

22. See Griffin, "Benedict XV and Cardinal Gibbons," 1–29.

23. Benedict XV, *Pacem*, 10.

24. Ibid., 1.

to promote love and forgiveness, since "the Gospel has not one law of charity for individuals and another for States."[25] Benedict XV thus anticipated the approach of more recent popes not only in his outright denunciation of war but also in his insistence that forgiveness is not a sidelight to formal post-conflict politics. Moreover, and perhaps most relevant to my project, he opens the path for whole peoples—not just politicians and soldiers—to assume social responsibility for repairing the sins of war.

Also of relevance for the deeply social and penitential approach of John Paul II is the Second Vatican Council and consequent ecclesial responses to structures of sin. Of course, the paradigmatic example comes in the Pastoral Constitution on the Church in the Modern World, *Gaudium et spes*. Its famous opening declares a kind of shared responsibility by which "the joy and hope, grief and aguish" of the whole world are taken on by "the followers of Christ."[26] The text also promotes the need for social analysis, since "the structure of affairs is flawed by the consequence of sin."[27] The breadth of practical topics tackled in the text—from economic inequality, to the scourge of war, to threats to marriage and the family—displayed a renewed engagement by which the church brings resources for the task of social repair. On the role of penance in this effort, the Dogmatic Constitution on the Church, *Lumen gentium*, is even more explicit. While Christ knew nothing of sin, "the Church, however, clasping sinners to her bosom, at once holy and always in need of purification, follows constantly the path of penance and renewal."[28] Coming out of the Council, a subtle but important connection seems to emerge: the desire to join the cause against sin in the social order impels the church to consider its own struggle against sin and to offer a resource that is at its very heart: the path of penance.

After the Council, the potential for synthesis between a social analysis of sin and the ecclesial resource of penance grew. Pfeil notes in particular the role of Latin America in bringing an awareness of the extent to which personal and social repair are intertwined. At Medellín, Colombia, in 1968 and Puebla, Mexico, in 1979, the bishops decry the social injustice of poverty and inequality, noting in these realities a call to self-examination and conversion. "We will not have a new continent without new and reformed structures, but above all there will be no new continent without new men,"

25. Ibid., 14.

26. *Gaudium et spes*, 1.

27. Ibid., 25

28. *Lumen gentium*, 8.

insisted the Medellín text.[29] At Puebla, the Latin American bishops echo a theme of John Paul II during his 1979 trip to Mexico by claiming that "the situation of social sinfulness" is "all the more serious because it exists in countries that call themselves Catholic and are capable of changing the situation."[30] The connection between social repair and the soul-searching work of penance had also been noted by the Synod of all the world's bishops in 1971 when, in their *Justice in the World* text, they acknowledge that "everyone who ventures to speak to people about justice must first be just in their eyes. Hence we must undertake an examination of the modes of acting and of the possessions and lifestyle found within the Church herself."[31] The post-Vatican II awareness of structural sin and political engagement thus need not be pitted against the vitality of ecclesial practices of self-examination and conversion.

Twentieth-century themes of structural sin and penance meet most dramatically in the pontificate of John Paul II. He was increasingly driven to describe sin in social terms. In 1998, just after a trip to Latin America, he wrote in his encyclical letter *Sollicitudo rei socialis*,

> "Sin" and "structures of sin" are categories which are seldom applied to the situation of the contemporary world. However, one cannot easily gain a profound understanding of the reality that confronts us unless we give a name to the root of the evils which afflict us.[32]

At the same time that this awareness was coming to the fore of his social teaching, John Paul II was in the midst of calling the church to penance in preparation for the Jubilee Year, as we will see. The thread connecting them was personal responsibility. The fact that a single individual may not *choose* to inflict a massive injustice, like poverty or slave labor conditions, does not eliminate responsibility for the sin. In fact, he argues specifically in *Sollicitudo* that "structures of sin" are "rooted in personal sin."[33] In explaining the link, the pope invoked his letter after the 1983 Synod on reconciliation and penance, in which he used expansive terms to describe personal responsibility for social sins, including not just direct acts but "laziness, fear, silence,

29. In Pfeil, "Toward an Understanding," 61.
30. Ibid., 85.
31. Ibid., 75.
32. John Paul II, *Sollicitudo rei socialis*, 36.
33. Ibid.

indifference" and even including "those who take refuge in the supposed impossibility of changing the world."[34]

For John Paul, even the "awareness" of suffering and injustice in distant parts of the world acquires "a moral connotation" and personal responsibility.[35] The pope here is moving beyond the traditional categories of cooperation with evil to measure guilt. Guilt, while not an unimportant concept, is not his main focus. As he insists again and again, the point is solidarity, "the firm and persevering determination to commit oneself to the common good," which is a "virtue" rooted in the fact that "we are all really responsible for all."[36] John Paul is explicit that, if pursued, solidarity brings a power of social repair that is productive of real peace—"opus solidaritatis pax"—and a reconciliation that in its depth is marked by "total gratuity."[37] Such virtue, of course, requires personal conversion and the recognition of our own individual participation in a kind of pathological solidarity that is on display in the world's structures of sin. For this reason, John Paul knew that it was not enough to outline a vision of social reform but that also needed was a visible program of penance.

John Paul II, the Penitent Pope

> As the Successor of Peter, I ask that in this year of mercy the Church, strong in the holiness which she receives from her Lord, should kneel before God and implore forgiveness for the past and present sins of her sons and daughters. All have sinned and none can claim righteousness before God (cf. 1 Kgs 8:46). . . . The Church is a communion of saints, but a solidarity in sin also exists among all the members of the People of God.[38]

With these words, the Vatican announced a "Day of Pardon," to be celebrated within a eucharistic liturgy at St. Peter's Basilica on the first Sunday of Lent, March 12, of the Jubilee Year 2000. Plans for such an event were long in the making—and not without opposition. As he began to prepare for the Jubilee Year, the pope, in 1994, held a consistory of all the church's

34. Ibid., *Reconciliatio et Penitentia*, 16.
35. Ibid., *Solicitudo rei socialis*, 38.
36. Ibid.
37. Ibid., 39, 40.
38. John Paul II, "'Day of Pardon' Presentation," 1.

cardinals, at which he proposed *Reflections on the Great Jubilee of the Year 2000*. Section 7 was given a familiar title, "Reconciliatio et Paenitentia," the same wording used in his exhortation following the 1983 Synod of Bishops. John Paul knew that some cardinals were concerned about whether the church should, *or even could*, admit sinfulness. In response, he wrote that repentance "will in no way do injury to the moral prestige of the Church, which will on the contrary emerge from it strengthened, since it will attest to its honesty and courage in recognizing mistakes committed by its members and, in a certain sense, in its name."[39] Even after receiving the pope's rationale, Secretary of State Angelo Sodano reported that "a number of venerable cardinals urge great caution, since it is an extremely difficult and touchy issue."[40] Most vehement was Cardinal Biffi of Bologna, Italy:

> The Church, if one views it as it truly is, has no sins, for it is "the whole Christ": its head is the Son of God, to whom no moral misconduct can be attributed. Nevertheless, the Church can adopt the feeling of sadness and pain appropriate to the personal misconduct of its members. . . . They are its sons, yet it does not assume their sins.[41]

The pope repeatedly granted the point: insofar as one sins, one acts outside of the communion whose bond is Christ himself. For this reason, John Paul spoke of the sins of the "sons and daughters" of the church, acknowledging that this, too, includes popes, bishops, and all the faithful. But the pope did not want the Jubilee gestures to be matters of theological debate. Even if the matter was "touchy," he was committed to acknowledging the "solidarity in sin" and, thus, moving to the third millennium "in a spirit of 'reconciliation and repentance.'"[42]

In his 1994 letter *Tertio Millennio Adveniente*, John Paul made his fullest and most public case for including a program of penance in Jubilee celebrations. There, he explained the roots of the Jubilee Year in the Old Testament. Every seventh year was to be a sabbatical in which slaves were freed, debts canceled, and soil left fallow and given rest—"all this was to be done in honor of God."[43] After seven sabbatical years, the following year (the fiftieth) called for even greater joy, jubilee, to celebrate God's care for

39. In Accattoli et al., *John Paul II*, 106.

40. Ibid., 107.

41. Ibid., 107–8.

42. Ibid., 103.

43. John Paul II, *Coming of the Third Millennium*, 12.

all by returning liberty and property to the dispossessed (Lev 25:10). John Paul noted that in the practice of Jubilee, "a kind of social doctrine began to emerge," a *restorative* one that offered "new possibilities" for communal life.[44] Christ himself proclaimed the Jubilee, the "year of favor from the Lord," when he returned to his home synagogue and read the Isaiah scroll that proclaims "good tidings to the afflicted" (Luke 4:18). In explaining the tradition, the pope then makes two observations particularly relevant to this chapter. First, he notes that the Jubilee is "a year for the remission of sins and of the punishments due to them."[45] The notion of canceling punishments, analogous to debts, helps explain why the pope's Jubilee gestures focus more on a gratuitous economy of forgiveness than on the work of reparation consequent to that gift. This is a point to which I will return. Second, in seeking a Jubilee full of "manifold conversions" and a "year of reconciliation," John Paul makes explicit reference both to the sacrament and to "extra-sacramental penance."[46] Indeed, it is in this category that we can see the greatest potential for application of the pope's strategy to the wider public arena. To make that case, I will first describe the penitential liturgy itself that began the Jubilee Lenten repentance, as well as the theological rationale given to it by John Paul II himself.

The March 12, 2000, Day of Pardon liturgy was a remarkable performance. In his comprehensive study of Protestant and Catholic penitence, Jeremy Bergen observes that "the image of the aging John Paul II on his knees in St. Peter's Basilica . . . remains perhaps the most widely received instance of ecclesial repentance to date."[47] The following day, in the *New York Times*, papal spokesman Joaquin Navarro-Valls was quoted as saying, "This is an entirely new thing. . . . I think it will take years for the Church to absorb it."[48] The provocative Mass began with the pope at Michelangelo's *Pietà* near the entrance of St. Peter's. Vested in purple, he prayed as a sign that the church, "like Mary," takes responsibility for her children. The pope then led the entrance procession as the Litany of Saints was sung, asking intercession to help "sinful brothers and sisters still on their pilgrim way." Though Sunday, the readings were typical for Ash Wednesday: Isaiah's suffering servant, upon whom was laid "the guilt of us all" (Isa 53:6); Paul's

44. Ibid., 13.
45. Ibid., 14.
46. Ibid.
47. Bergen, *Ecclesial Repentance*, 115.
48. Ibid.

exhortation to "be reconciled to God . . . who made him who did not know sin to be sin, so that in him we might become the righteousness of God" (2 Cor 5:20–21); and the brief Markan version of the temptation of Jesus, whom the Spirit sent "into the desert" (Mark 1:12). Placing the penitential liturgy on a Sunday seemed to indicate John Paul's desire that penance and joy, work and gift, reparation and resurrection, not be separated.

Indeed, the pope focused his homily on the great gift of the incarnation and on God's acts of love toward sinners, which elicit from us the desire to make a "profound examination of conscience" to acknowledge sins of the past and the "objective responsibility which Christians share as members of the Mystical Body." The pope also emphasized that "the recognition of past wrongs serves to reawaken our consciences" to "our responsibilities as Christians for the evils of today," and "to the compromises of the present, opening the way to conversion for everyone." John Paul invoked the mercy God offers to all "prodigal" children who return and say, "Father, I have sinned" (Luke 15:18). He closed by recalling again St. Paul, who experienced personally the "dazzling power" of Christ to make reconciliation possible, and by entrusting the Jubilee Year to Mary, "Mother of Forgiveness."

The most dramatic ritual of the Mass came in the Prayers of the Faithful, which were transformed into a "Universal Prayer" that included seven confessions delivered by seven members of the Roman Curia. The Dean of the College of Cardinals, Bernardin Gantin of Benin, began with a confession for sins "in general," expressing a "conscious and deep sorrow" and seeking a "purification of memory" leading to conversion. As with all seven confessions, a period of silence followed, broken by a prayer of the pope and the singing of the "Kyrie eleison." During the Kyrie, as a symbol of exposing darkness in the church's past, one flame was lit on a seven-branched candlestick placed before the fifteenth-century crucifix traditionally used during Jubilee years. The second confession was given by Cardinal Joseph Ratzinger, for "sins committed in the service of truth," a reference to the Inquisition and other investigations that "used methods not in keeping with the Gospel." The third confession, for sins harming "the unity of the Body of Christ," was made by Cardinal Roger Etchegaray and referenced historic failures in "fraternal charity" toward Protestants and Orthodox Christians. Next, Cardinal Edward Cassidy confessed "sins against the people of Israel." The prayer of response, the very words John Paul II placed in the Western Wall in Jerusalem during his Jubilee trip there, was less specific in its indictment than many Jews desired, but it did beg God's forgiveness and an opening toward "genuine brotherhood with the people of the Covenant."

The fifth confession focused on sins against ethnic and religious minorities and was delivered by Archbishop Stephen Hamao of Japan. The pope prayed that such acts, which reflected "a mentality of power" and showed "contempt for cultures," might give way to mercy in relationships. The sixth confession was made by Cardinal Francis Arinze of Nigeria and was directed at sins "against the dignity of women," whose role in the "unity of the human family" has too often been violated by "attitudes of rejection and exclusion." The consequent "acts of discrimination," the pope noted, also have been manifest in historic racism as well. The seventh and final confession addressed sins "against the fundamental rights of the person." Archbishop François-Xavier Nguyễn Văn Thuận, president of the Pontifical Council for Justice and Peace, focused this category on abortion and those who "abuse the promise of biotechnology and distort the aims of science." The pope's prayer used the account in Matthew 25 to connect the "little ones" killed by abortion to "the hungry, the thirsty and the naked, the persecuted, the imprisoned," all the poor who have suffered "acts of injustice." After a final prayer to conclude the litany of confessions, the pope engaged in what would become the iconic moment: embracing and kissing the crucifix, "as a sign of penance and veneration." The Mass then continued to the Liturgy of the Eucharist, with a final blessing designed specifically for the occasion, titled by the Vatican "Commitment for a conversion of life." In that sending forth, John Paul employed the "never again" motif to name each of the sins confessed and to "awaken in the whole Church . . . renewed fidelity to the perennial message of the Gospel."

As Bergen notes, reaction to the Day of Pardon was immediate and massive. In general, secular media outlets gave a positive assessment of the pope's "courageous and historic declaration," as the *New York Times* put it.[49] Some complained that the confessions were too general, or omitted certain groups, or were not tied to particular reforms. One response, by *Los Angeles Times* columnist Nicolaus Mills, connected the pope's plea to the rise in public apologies, but wondered whether it met the criteria of being "directed at whomever has been damaged" and being "accompanied by reparations," a critique I will address below.[50] Among church commenta-

---

49. *New York Times*, "The Pope's Apology," March 14, 2000, http://www.nytimes.com/2000/03/14/opinion/the-pope-s-apology.html.

50. Mills, "Modern Notion of a Public Apology," 3.

tors, other reservations were brewing. Even before the Day of Pardon, Mary Ann Glendon had wondered whether the *mea culpas* might be manipulated by enemies of the church, for whom "no apology will ever be enough until Catholics apologize themselves into nonexistence."[51] Significant response to the event itself also centered on the aforementioned question of ascribing sin to the church. On this subject, answers on both sides emerged. Cardinal Biffi argued that the confessions might jeopardize the principle that sins are "ontologically extra-ecclesial."[52] An editorial in *America* proposed that "if we are the church, then the church has sinned."[53] Taken as a whole, then, the range of reaction in the secular and Catholic world indicated the significance of John Paul's gestures—a nerve had clearly been struck—with some worrying he had gone too far and others frustrated that he had not gone far enough.

For the purposes of my project, the historic importance of the Day of Pardon does not consist so much in how it advanced the question of whether the church can *sin*. More to the point is the way it displayed the teaching that the church can *do penance*. This doctrine was invoked explicitly in the Second Vatican Council, when the opening section of *Lumen gentium* concluded by linking penance to the nature of the church, "at once holy and always in need of purification."[54] This principle is important for my project in two ways, both of which received insufficient attention in the reaction to the Jubilee Day of Pardon. First, the pope's ecclesial performance made clear that persons can do penance for sins they did not commit. The description of sins even from centuries ago can name proclivities that we all share—as when John Paul named the "mentality of power" or "attitudes of exclusion"—and thus provide an opportunity to lament, take responsibility for, and seek to repair damage done by sins directly committed by others. I will return to this notion of "corporate penance" when I suggest its application to the contemporary burden of repair after war and how a whole people—who might prefer to ascribe war's sins to others—can share penance with soldiers and political leaders.

Second, and related, emphasizing penance as the proper communal response to the sins of its members avoids the problem of "collective guilt." The pope was keenly aware of the problematic role this notion played in

51. Glendon, "Contrition in the Age of Spin Control."
52. In Dulles, "Should the Church Repent?"
53. *America*, "Asking Forgiveness," 3.
54. *Lumen gentium*, 8.

the history of anti-Judaism, placing blame on Jews as a whole for the death of Jesus. Because of this, he was careful not to allow the idea of corporate penance to blur lines of material culpability. In fact, just this concern was part of the reason why John Paul qualified his concept of social sin with the aforementioned proviso that "sin is properly an act of the person." Put another way, preferring corporate penance to collective guilt opens space for a more forward-looking and constructive response to sin, which is precisely why the Day of Pardon was designed not to judge the past but to help the church "cross the threshold of the new millennium."[55] That is, in order for the church to experience the purification and renewal necessary for its mission of social repair—a mission so prominent in the Jubilee tradition—John Paul saw the liturgy as the moment to "inaugurate a journey of conversion and change."[56]

Bringing Penance to the World Stage

Accattoli describes the capacity for asking forgiveness—a trait on its fullest display in the Day of Pardon—as the "decisive innovation of John Paul II's pontificate."[57] And it began early. His election came just twenty days after he participated in a historic reconciliation between bishops of two countries, Poland and Germany, whose people had suffered the scourge of the Holocaust and the Second World War. That effort, too, had its roots in Vatican II when, as the Council ended in 1965, the Polish bishops—including Wojtyła, archbishop of Krakow—decided to mark the one-thousand-year anniversary of Christianity in Poland with a request for the German bishops to attend the celebration. That would mean contending with the past, and the letter minces no words in describing their country during German occupation as "studded with concentration camps in which the chimneys of the crematoria smoked day and night," leading to "the extermination of six million Polish citizens, the majority of Jewish origin," along with two thousand priests and five bishops who were killed in the camps. And yet "in spite of it all . . . let us try to forget! No polemics; no continuation of the cold war, but the beginning of a dialogue. . . . In this very Christian and the same

---

55. John Paul II, "'Day of Pardon' Presentation," 3.

56. Ibid., 4.

57. Accattoli, "A Pope Who Begs Forgiveness," in Accattoli et al., *John Paul II*, 89.

time very human spirit, we extend our hands to you, seated on the benches of a Council about to end, forgiving and asking forgiveness."[58]

The troubling dimensions of the call "to forget" reveal the later maturation of Wojtyła's approach to reconciliation, in which he will emphasize "purification of memory," a process of shared remembering that takes place for the purpose of healing. I will explore that concept below but here wish simply to note that, while the invitation to reconciliation was quickly accepted by the German bishops, it was not well received by the Polish government, which responded that the Poles had nothing for which to ask forgiveness. An official response from the bishops, thought to have been penned by Wojtyła, grants the disproportionate sins suffered by Poles but also invokes the phrase "there are no innocents." Interestingly, Wojtyła connects that "Christian principle" to the literary work of Albert Camus, adding to the broad human appeal of the idea of solidarity in sin. The ongoing dialogue between Polish and German Catholics continued, culminating in a September 1978 conference in Germany, less than a week before the death of John Paul I. Unaware of his pending election, Cardinal Wojtyła preached a homily during the visit in which he explicitly tied their efforts at reconciliation to the approaching dawn of the third millennium and the need to "heal the wounds of the past."[59]

The experience of leading a specific expedition for reconciliation set the stage for the new pope to bring this message to the world. It would be impossible to catalog here all of the expressions of repentance performed by John Paul II, but I will note several that have direct bearing on the political arena, particularly in the context of repairing the damage of war. He began the penitential lament of war in a city ravaged by many intra-Christian conflicts in history, Vienna. There, in 1983, he mourned "the dark and terrifying events which are incompatible with the spirit of humanity and the Gospel of Jesus Christ," noting that the involvement of "devout Christians" in those wars "is a depressing thought" that must lead us "to confess" that we have "burdened ourselves with great guilt."[60] The pope's use of "we" at Vienna raises again the nature of responsibility for sin. I have already noted that those not directly involved in a sin can nonetheless participate in the logic behind the sin, but here the pope seems to go further and suggest that unless penance is done, the sins of Christians *then* remain the responsibil-

58. Accattoli, *When a Pope Asks Forgiveness*, 49.

59. Ibid., 51.

60. Ibid., 140.

ity of Christians *now*. This is *not* the *transfer* of guilt for a single sin from one set of persons to another. It is more akin to a sharing of original sin, inherited in particular ways from the communities to which we belong. Indeed, the pope alluded to the relevance of communal culture when he noted on the fiftieth anniversary of the Second World War that it took place "on a continent which stood under the influence of the Gospel and the Church longer than any other."[61] Of course, connections across space and time hold unique relevance for the church as "the mystical body of Christ," but I will argue that key elements of shared responsibility for sin extend to all traditions and cultures.

If solidarity in sin extended for John Paul II across the boundaries of space and time, then he went further still in 1992 when he asked forgiveness from the dead who had been victims of the Conquest. He traveled to Santo Domingo—the very site where Dominicans like Las Casas had decried the domination of native peoples—on the five hundredth anniversary of the arrival of Columbus in the Americas. Calling his journey a "pilgrimage" and "an act of atonement," he reflected that an unceasing "plea for forgiveness is directed above all to the original inhabitants of the New World, to the Indians—and also to those dragged here from Africa for forced labor as slaves."[62] Here we see his penitential stance cut also across the border of life and death, using "we" to ask murdered victims for forgiveness. The inclusion of such a plea reflects the mystical elements of his approach and reflects the influence of theologian Hans Urs von Balthasar, who had emphasized the "burden of the dead."[63] The plea also signals that ecclesial penance cannot be reduced to a program of social repair, though a reverence for the agency of those killed also has striking contemporary applicability. As I will suggest, acknowledging the relevance of the dead would go a long way toward a more healthy approach to a moral reckoning for recent American wars in Iraq and Afghanistan.

A final example in which John Paul's penitence meets the wounds of war will help direct us toward the practical results that he achieved in stoking reconciliation. In 1995, the pope traveled to Slovakia, the site of seventeenth-century massacres of Protestants by Catholics and Catholics by Protestants. The reason for his trip was ostensibly to canonize three of the Catholics killed in one of the ugly episodes, a move that angered

---

61. Accattoli, "A Pope Who Begs Forgiveness," in Accattoli et al., *John Paul II*, 98.

62. Ibid., 100.

63. See Accattoli, *When a Pope Asks Forgiveness*, 3.

Protestants, who saw it as opening old wounds and laying blame at their feet. But in his homily, John Paul reversed the entire dynamic at work in his visit. After noting the refusal of the three martyrs to violate their conscience, he referenced "many other people" who also suffered. Then the key words, "How can we fail to acknowledge the spiritual greatness of the twenty-four members of the Evangelical Churches who were killed at Presov?"[64] Then came the key action. After the liturgy, the pope broke with the schedule and walked in silence and rain to nearby Presov to pray at the monument of those martyrs who refused to acknowledge the papal authority he now exercised. The symbolic gesture had consequences, with the Lutheran bishop and others who had protested his visit publicly acknowledging the complicity of their communities and taking steps toward healing the painful memories that were still operative among Slovakians.[65] The pope also opened dialogue when, during a similar canonization homily in 1995 in the Czech Republic, he made the scope of his program explicit: "Today I, the pope of the Church of Rome, in the name of all Catholics, ask forgiveness . . ."[66] These episodes bore fruit in consequent dialogue and gestures of reciprocity amid still-tense settings, displaying the capacity for single acts of repentance to evoke a broader commitment to reconciliation.

The historic penitential gestures of John Paul II—sometimes described as if it were one long "apology tour"—can be misinterpreted if seen as preoccupied with past events where the main actors are no longer on the stage to be held accountable. In fact, the pope did plea for forgiveness and accountability in light of current political crises. The clearest example came in the midst of Rwandan genocide in 1994, when John Paul lamented the killings, including the role of many Catholics, and encouraged a "moral reawakening" that included the justice by which perpetrators must "answer for their crimes."[67] Still, the pope can rightly be faulted for a lack of action in contemporary crises, especially in regard to repression in Latin America and the response to clergy sexual abuse, which will be addressed below. Indeed, the forward-poised dimension of his penitential gestures consists not in their timeliness but rather in their ability to create what John Paul II himself called "new relationship[s] and active collaboration" propelled

---

64. Ibid., 147.

65. Accattoli, "A Pope Who Begs Forgiveness," in Accattoli et al., *John Paul II*, 100.

66. Ibid., 146.

67. Accattoli, *When a Pope Asks Forgiveness*, 214.

by "the mercy of God."[68] The language of renewal in the wake of penance recalls the theme of my previous chapter, which described a Thomistic approach to confession as ordered toward the generation of fresh commitments to right relationship. Here, that outcome is broadened beyond the experience of one penitent in the sacrament and proposed for use by whole peoples. The success of that enterprise can be measured in its reception and employment in political and ecclesial communities of diverse contexts. Thus, having described the particulars of John Paul's pontificate of repentance, I will move in the next section to a brief treatment of the dynamic it unleashed on the world stage.

Unleashing the Dynamic of Repentance: Responses to John Paul II

While the pope had been building the case for penance during the twenty-one years leading up to the Jubilee, it was only with the Day of Pardon that a cascade of efforts clearly emerged in local and regional religious communities of the world. Early in the new millennium, the Italian journal *Il Regno* published a "Diario del perdono" to catalog all of the initiatives that had begun in response to the penitential liturgy in St. Peter's. It was an impressive list: twenty-three bishops' conferences and many individual bishops had issued calls to repentance on a variety of matters.[69] The Australian bishops addressed relationships with Aboriginal peoples, hardly a wound only in the past. Several European conferences begged forgiveness from Jews. The Dominicans, Jesuits, and Franciscans all issued Jubilee calls to renewal in areas like interreligious dialogue. In Maryland, Cardinal William Keeler went to his Basilica to admit in front of black Catholics that priests, religious orders, and even the United States' first bishop, John Carroll, owned slaves and that racism has "gnawed at the moral fiber of our nation, our community, and our church."[70] Archbishop Michael Sheehan of Santa Fe, New Mexico, lamented the historic mistreatment of Native Americans, but he also lamented the more recent role of civic leaders, including many Catholics, in sustaining and expanding a prison system that too often impedes reconciliation. In Los Angeles, Cardinal Roger Mahony asked the

68. Quoted in ibid., 225.

69. Accattoli, "A Pope Who Begs Forgiveness," in Accattoli et al., *John Paul II*, 114–15. See also Bergen, *Ecclesial Repentance*, 144–45.

70. Biemer, "US Catholic Hierarchy Asks Forgiveness for Past Sins," 1.

forgiveness of gay persons whose civil rights the church had undercut through tolerance of homophobia. To the many other examples of Catholic repentance were added initiatives from Orthodox, Anglican, Presbyterian, Methodist, and Pentecostal communities, as well as Buddhist, Muslim, and Baha'i statements of communal lament for wrongdoing.[71]

What all of the above efforts have in common, of course, is their religious character. This is not to say that each of them did not also have wider implications for the many laypersons shaping institutions and cultures. Yet, if I wish to show most clearly the relevance of penance for politics, I need to point to the way that John Paul's gestures directly impacted structures of public life. Precisely this example is on display in the successful Jubilee effort to seek relief for highly indebted poor countries. What is noteworthy about the Vatican's participation in the Jubilee 2000 debt campaign is that throughout the endeavor, the pope continued to rely on religious tradition and the biblical vision of Jubilee to forge connections with the many secular groups participating in and being lobbied by the campaign. Moreover, the penitential rationale for the granting of debt forgiveness by wealthy nations carried substantive political weight in the victory achieved. Both of these dimensions make the debt relief effort illuminating for my own project to employ a theological, penitential rationale to social repair in the public arena.

The two figures most widely associated with Jubilee debt relief were John Paul II and the rock star Bono. The two had met in September 1999, during what Vatican analyst John Allen calls "an unusual meeting" in which the pope addressed and explicitly endorsed the campaign being led by notables from the world of entertainment and economics.[72] In his comments to the group, John Paul noted that "today's world has need of a Jubilee experience" that can help restore "the original harmony which God had given to his creation." He wanted his words echoed to leaders in "especially the most powerful nations," to whom he asked a pointed question: "Why so many hesitations?" The pope knew that the Jubilee 2000 debt campaign needed help in securing the victories they had begun to achieve. Earlier in the summer, Bono had presented a petition with more than seventeen million signatures to German Chancellor Gerhard Schroeder and the leaders of a G7 Summit in Cologne. To the pope, he presented his signature

---

71. Accattoli, "A Pope Who Begs Forgiveness," in Accattoli et al., *John Paul II*, 114–15; Bergen, *Ecclesial Repentance*, 144–45.

72. Allen, *Future Church*, 258.

sunglasses, making possible another of the most iconic moments of John Paul's pontificate. The image of the rocker and the pope, the latter flashing what Bono called "the wickedest smile," would become a global symbol of the "intriguing symbiosis" that drove the debt relief campaign.[73]

Allen's description of the symbiosis emphasizes that, more than fame, the duo achieved "remarkable success"—twenty-three nations were granted debt reduction or cancellation, and over $100 billion in relief was promised.[74] In the ensuing years, this promise was scrutinized and given mixed reviews for implementation, though in 2005 the campaign continued to put pressure on the G8 and yielded a further commitment to debt relief. The point to emphasize here is the extent to which the pope—and the church that he mobilized, including especially religious orders—was able to stoke political action. The movement of which they were a part understood "the multilevel character of the globalized world," spurring action within governments, financial institutions, transnational networks, and grassroots actors.[75] Indeed, as Allen further notes, "The Jubilee 2000 campaign suggests that Catholicism still has tremendous social capital that, if invested wisely, can help change the world."[76]

While the impact of Pope John Paul II on the Jubilee debt campaign has been widely noted, rarely is it tied explicitly to his ecclesial gestures of penitence or even to the larger culture of self-examination that he fostered. And yet, this link is important. Even the linguistic parallel of debt *forgiveness* points to the way that lines between secular politics and sacred principles were thinned by the Jubilee mentality promoted by the pope. But, more than a mentality, John Paul *enacted* themes of pardon and penitence so that his call for debt relief came with a moral authority and integrity of example. This illustrates once again that the pope's contribution in his gestures of penance was not so much the clarification of historical errors as the presentation of a way, a strategy for addressing any injustice. Bergen characterizes this as a move "from the prophetic critique of others to a penitent self-examination," and I would argue that this shift was key to the success of the Jubilee 2000 debt campaign.[77] Indeed, there are no shortages of social justice campaigns brimming with prophetic critique, but this

73. Ibid., 259.

74. Ibid., 258.

75. Ibid., 260.

76. Ibid.

77. Bergen, *Ecclesial Repentance*, 147.

effort—lodged firmly in a Jubilee context of repentance and repair—has stood out as particularly effective. I am not naïve to the many factors beyond the pope's role, but the success does point to a kind of dynamic—I might even say power—that can be unleashed by a penitential approach. Other strategies, such as a rights-based or interest-group approach, are important in holding structures of power to account. But a penitential movement is better able to invite a mutuality and participatory response of shared action. The genius of John Paul II is that he was able to turn what many saw as "mea culpas" into something more—the capacity for "nostra culpas" and for communal action ordered to social repair.

A Failed Moment: Penance in the Wake of the Sex Abuse Crisis

A treatment of the impact of John Paul's penitential approach on the global stage would not be honest if it did not confront the sexual abuse crisis, which seized worldwide attention not long after the Jubilee Year was complete. Beginning in January 2002, the *Boston Globe* ran stories with headlines such as this one: "Scores of Priests Involved in Sex Abuse Cases: Settlements Kept Scope of Issue out of Public Eye."[78] The revelations in Boston were matched with stories and investigations in the rest of the country, and soon the American church was rocked by a scandal of epic proportion. Much critical attention has been given to the way in which the bishops handled the crisis. Anselma Dolcich-Ashley, for example, has pointed out that while statements of apology began to proliferate throughout 2002, the bishops viewed the crisis mainly as "a problem of individual sinful priests."[79] Such an approach displayed what Stephen Pope called "exculpatory strategies" that acknowledge regret in general terms but do not take responsibility for specific cases.[80]

At their historic 2002 meeting in Dallas, which passed the *Charter for the Protection of Children and Young People*, the bishops seemed poised to "articulate a sense of their cooperation in the crisis."[81] In his Opening Address there, USCCB president Wilton Gregory issued this reminder to his brother bishops:

78. Robinson et al., "Scores of Priests Involved in Sex Abuse Cases."
79. Dolcich-Ashley, "Precept, Rights and Ecclesial Governance," 27.
80. Pope, "Accountability and Sexual Abuse," 76.
81. Dolcich-Ashley, "Precept, Rights and Ecclesial Governance," 54.

We are the ones . . . who allowed priest abusers to remain in ministry. . . . *We are the ones* . . . who chose not to report the criminal actions of priests to the authorities. . . . *We are the ones* who worried
more about the possibility of scandal than bringing about the kind
of openness that helps prevent abuse. *And we are the ones* who at
times responded to victims and their families as adversaries and
not as suffering members of the church.[82]

But, as Dolcich-Ashley points out, the expressions that emerged in the
months and years to follow were more akin to "expressions of sympathy,
rather than robust apologies."[83] She uses the work of Nick Smith on the
meaning of apologies to suggest that better than saying "I am sorry" is saying "I was wrong," which "brings a greater measure of clarity and precision,
and makes possible a deeper dialogue into the causal factors of the injury."[84]
On this point, Dolcich-Ashley laments that moral categories, like Liguori's
levels of cooperation with evil, were functionally absent from the ecclesial
response. In fact, proficiency with these principles of social analysis was
better displayed by lawyers and judges than by the leaders of the tradition
from which those principles came.[85] Lastly, her analysis of the apologies
concludes that too many "come across as free and gratuitous gifts rather
than as obligations of justice,"[86] as if the bishop is going out of his way for
the sake of victims. Much more appropriate, concludes Dolcich-Ashley,
would have been a response more closely tethered to Catholic sacramental practice: "The penitent must accept guilt for offenses, identify them by
number and kind, express true contrition, and take up a penance designed
to promote healing of injuries and relationships."[87]

I do not aim here at a comprehensive analysis of the abuse crisis, but
given the context of papal apology in this chapter, it is important to note
the problematic nature of that element in the American response. And I
agree with the conclusions of Dolcich-Ashley on those apologies—with
one caveat, which actually comes from the debate surrounding John Paul
II's Jubilee Day of Pardon. Though the word *apology* was and is used to describe those gestures, the Vatican itself resisted the term. Part of the reason

82. Gregory, "Presidential Address" cited in ibid., 54–55, emphasis added.
83. Dolcich-Ashley, "Precept, Rights and Ecclesial Governance," 64.
84. Ibid., 62.
85. See ibid., 48.
86. Ibid., 61.
87. Ibid., 58.

was to avoid the misinterpretation that the pleas were being directed at victims when, in fact, the confessions were made to God. While this may seem to make the problem worse—were victims being left out?—actually, it illuminates the purpose of those public acts, which were designed not to replace but to evoke and provoke concrete acts of reconciliation and repair. Public apologies often function best this way, not as a substitute for the precise accounting that also must be made to particular victims, but as a more general establishment of a penitential stance. In this way, the problem with American bishops was not so much the public lamentations but rather—and here I am in full agreement with Dolcich-Ashley—the fact that the lamentations were not followed to their *full* penitential end, including taking responsibility for each case and making reparation—not only restitution, but the full Thomistic sense of *satisfaction*—to each victim and to the community.

The question of penance—and its absence as the paradigm of response to the sexual abuse crisis—raises a final point that brings the role of John Paul II into sharp focus. In April 2002, three months after the eruption of the crisis, the pope called the cardinals of the United States to Rome for a private meeting. In the official communiqué reporting the results of the April 23 dialogue, the Vatican listed the following recommendation:

> It would be fitting for the Bishops of the United States Conference of Catholic Bishops to ask the faithful to join them in observing a national day of prayer and penance, in reparation for the offenses perpetrated and in prayer to God for the conversion of sinners and the reconciliation of victims.[88]

A specific proposal for just such a penitential day, to be held on September 14, the feast of the Exaltation of the Cross, did make it to the agenda of the Dallas meeting in 2002, taken up at the end of the day on which the bishops had passed the Charter. But, in the debate, a number of complicating factors were raised, ostensibly not related to the substance of the plan but to the date. Cardinal Law of Boston noted that this was a celebratory feast day in his diocesan Holy Cross Cathedral. Many others objected that the date was too close to the first anniversary of the September 11 attacks, with many memorials planned around the nation. In the end, as Jerry Filteau of Catholic News Service reported, the bishops decided to "commit

---

88. Vatican, "Final Communiqué," April 24, 2002 (http://www.vatican.va/roman_curia/cardinals/documents/rc_cardinals_20020424_final-communique_en.html).

themselves to prayer and penance" a month earlier, on August 14 and 15, and "simply invite other Catholics to join in."[89]

A number of relevant insights can already be made before exploring the ultimate fate of the scaled-down attempt at communal penance. First, little coverage was given to the idea of a proposed day of penance. Almost universal focus had been given to the Charter and its measure to identify and permanently "dismiss from the clerical state" any priest guilty of any act of sexual abuse of minors at any time in the past.[90] The adopted strategy to identify and expunge was working in the media, providing Americans with the kind of action worthy of media attention. This is not to say that removal from ministry was not an important element of a plan to protect children, but only that that this strategy entirely overshadowed any call to communal penance. Second, being unable to agree on the September 14 national day of prayer and penance, the bishops decided to "express support for local options" to display repentance for sexual abuse.[91] While not itself problematic, this decision was in some dissonance with the overall approach at Dallas, which indeed had just yielded a national charter. Nonetheless, the bishops were at least committing themselves to acts of penance and inviting the Catholic community to join.

Except that August 14 came and went with little evidence of communal prayer and penance. Revisiting chronicles of the crisis in 2002, one finds the troubling absence of any widespread effort within the USCCB infrastructure to plan or promote events encouraging broad participation in penitential actions. Later in 2002, in a comments section attached to the Filteau story, one observer asked this pointed question: "I thought there was supposed to be a national day of penance. Whatever happened to that?"[92] To be sure, some diocesan events were held. In Chicago, a liturgy was led by Cardinal Francis George in Holy Name Cathedral. The Archdiocese of Minneapolis-St. Paul held a Holy Hour on August 14, 2002, and, in Portland, Oregon, Bishop John Vlazny used the opportunity to reintroduce the traditional practice of "Ember Days," instituted nearly a thousand years ago by Pope Gregory VII to set aside during Advent and Lent days of commu-

89. Filteau, "Bishops to Fast, Pray," 1.

90. *Charter for the Protection of Children and Young People*, Article 5. This article does contain the proviso that an elderly priest be allowed to "live a life of prayer and penance," though he would not be allowed "to celebrate Mass publicly, to wear clerical garb, or to present himself publicly as a priest."

91. Filteau, "Bishops to Fast, Pray," 1.

92. Ibid.

nal fasting and penance. Other dioceses, too, held liturgies, some of which, such as that in Portland, Maine, have become annual events. But there was, and is, no national day of penance in any sense of the term.

How do we assess this failure in light of the explicit recommendation that emerged from their meeting with Pope John Paul II? On one hand, it is quite reasonable to expect that such a day be instituted. On the official calendar of the Catholic Church in the United States, January 22 is a Day of Penance and Prayer marking the anniversary of the Supreme Court's *Roe v. Wade* decision. On this day, the *General Instruction of the Roman Missal* directs presiders to wear purple vestments "as an appropriate liturgical observance for this day." During the campaign in opposition to contraceptive and abortifacient regulations of the 2010 Affordable Care Act, the bishops instituted on every Friday of the year a day of fasting and abstinence for "Life, Marriage and Religious Liberty." These are important causes, but they do raise the question of whether communal penance is being invoked to separate Catholics from the sins of public "others" rather than to lament, take responsibility for, and repair the sins of our community. Here we see the relevance of Bergen's distinction between prophetic critique and self-examination, the latter of which was on clear display in the Jubilee gestures of John Paul II but was perhaps less visible in the bishops' activities.

On the other hand, this is not a simple case of American bishops once again deviating from the directives of Rome. In the text of his address to the U.S. cardinals on April 23, 2002, the pope did not make explicit their need for public acts of communal penitence. He did express his own "profound sense of solidarity" with victims and the need for "a purification of the entire Catholic community" by turning to God for the power to seek forgiveness and reconciliation.[93] Thus, we do not know the precise origin of the recommendation, included in the final communiqué, for a national day of prayer and penance. Moreover, it is easy to see how the intense legal and financial drama unfolding rapidly in 2002 made communal penance a less than popular element of the response. Reacting to the original proposal for a day of penance, one online commenter inveighed that the bishops move abusive priests "from one parish to another, refuse to resign, try to stiff the victims on settlements, want the parishioners to pay the cost of the lawsuits, and now want me to do their penance for them to make the 'ouchie' all good again. Sorry—I'll do penance for my own sins, not theirs!"[94] In this climate,

---

93. John Paul II, "Address of John Paul II to the Cardinals of the United States."

94. Filteau, "Bishops to Fast, Pray," 1.

it was difficult not to see penance as distracting from the "real" business at hand, which seemed to be mollifying public outrage and limiting financial damage. No doubt, the full incorporation of a penitential ethic may have cost many millions more than even the mind-numbing price tag exacted by the scandals, which was estimated in 2013 at more than $2.5 billion.[95]

But if exculpatory strategies were pursued to mitigate financial and criminal liability, it is now clear that such an approach usually just delayed the impact. Moreover, the lack of a comprehensive and institutional approach to penance in the wake of the scandals deprived the Catholic community of resources that could have served the cause of justice and thus promoted deeper reconciliation. Communal penance could have also helped demonstrate more effectively a truth that, interestingly, John Paul II explicitly did raise in his address to the cardinals: the culpability of our whole culture. His reference to a "deep-seated crisis of sexual morality" surely cannot be dismissed in an age in which the sexualization of adolescents—the precise age group most victimized in clerical abuse—is commonplace in mainstream media.[96] This point was raised by some bishops but was dismissed as yet another attempt to deflect personal responsibility. But if it had been set in a context more clearly penitential and committed to self-examination—one that included more of what Dolcich-Ashley noted was absent—the call to the entire community to participate in the repair of abusive relationships would have been more inviting.

Responsibility for the failure to incorporate communal penance more robustly does not rest only with the bishops. Indeed, the pope himself could have been more demonstrative in seeking the kind of witness he had cultivated in the Jubilee gestures, although, even in the two-year interval, his health had deteriorated. Interestingly, the pope's gestures did re-emerge a decade later at a 2012 liturgy for abuse victims, led by the Vatican prefect for bishops, using the model of seven pleas for forgiveness and the lighting of seven candles before the crucifix. Acts of this nature, especially when tethered to reform and to justice for victims, express not only lament but responsibility, a principle in short supply in the response to the crisis. My goal here is not to ask if a different "strategy" might have "worked" for the church: the extent of pathology and suffering was so great that its emergence could be nothing but painful. The best we can do now is to ask how, in such crises, the response to moral evil and human suffering can be

95. Grossman, "Clergy Sex Abuse Settlements Top $2.5 Billion Nationwide."

96. John Paul II, "Address to the Cardinals of the United States."

crafted so that the restoration of right relationships still remains a practical hope. And though the Catholic community missed an opportunity, I will argue that another scandal, also of epic proportion, is unfolding before our eyes. I refer to the crisis of suicide among U.S. soldiers, who are taking their own lives at alarming rates upon their return to a society that ostensibly extols them as heroes. Before showing the applicability of penitential strategies for that crisis, I will conclude this chapter by deepening the concept of communal penance that drove the Jubilee gestures of John Paul II.

Communal Penance and Theo-politics

To this point, my suggestion that gestures of communal penance are an important element of social repair has been rooted in the capacity for such gestures to evoke and produce widening commitments to reconciliation and justice. But, even if shown to be constructive as a strategy, communal penance is not without serious critics. In this final section I will address three of the most profound criticisms and defend the application of this approach to contemporary social challenges. The first criticism challenges the capacity of a community to be an agent of repentance. This perspective was voiced by the online commentator who wrote, "I'll do penance for my own sins, not theirs!" While I have noted that Catholic tradition promotes penance for the sins of others, I have not fully developed the rationale for the principle nor defended its deployment beyond the church. A second problem is that I have consistently used the term *penance* to describe the Jubilee gestures of John Paul II, yet those actions—most notably the Day of Pardon liturgy—did not explicitly speak to the matter of reparation. Given my own definition of penance as *practices through which persons lament, take responsibility for, and seek to repair the wounds that are caused by sin,* how can I justify using his approach as a form of concrete social repair? Finally, a consistent challenge to John Paul II came from those wary of the value of bringing up the wounds of a painful past—some thinking it sidestepped present sins and others that it had no practical value for the future. In response, I will develop the conceptual role of *memory* in a penitential approach to social repair. In addressing each of these items, I will attempt to highlight the social relevance of communal penance not only in the church but in the wider political arena. In this way, I will be ready for the final three chapters, in which I propose the penitential ethic.

In preparing for John Paul's Jubilee gestures, the International Theological Commission (ITC) released, in 1999, *Memory and Reconciliation: The Church and the Faults of the Past* (hereafter MR). MR presents the case for penance as a participatory enterprise, including but extending beyond the actors with specific culpability for sins. The case for this position begins with the Hebrew Scriptures and the common motif of confessing "the sins of the fathers."[97] "This is how the Jews prayed," MR states, and "the Church imitates their example."[98] In the New Testament, confessions for the sins of ancestors is gone, but a strong sense of corporate identity remains, which can even be seen in the words of the Lord's Prayer to "forgive *us our* trespasses, as *we* forgive those who trespass against *us*" (Luke 11:4; cf. Matt 6:12).[99] MR reiterates that John Paul's gestures are not a transfer of guilt across space or time and could not, for example, remove the need for confession and restitution incumbent on persons who have sinned. Rather, a focus on the "solidarity in sin" can deepen the awareness of responsibility in such persons and extend an awareness of responsibility to others who might not have imagined their complicity. Nor did the pope's actions promote "collective guilt." As Bergen notes, citing Bradford Hinze, a community such as the church "need not be collectively guilty in a 'fully volitional' sense to be collectively responsible and accountable, and to repent."[100]

The notion of communal responsibility may have strong *bona fides* in theological rationale, but pertinent to my project is its relevance for political community. Put another way, it is one thing to ascribe a singular identity to the church, a community constituted across space and time by Christ, but nations are another matter. This observation is correct, and MR notes "the difference between the Church as a mystery of grace and every human society in time."[101] But then comes a reference to "exemplarity" and to John Paul's own explicit claim that the penitential witness can "overflow as illumination and support for the decisions and actions of civil society," in particular of "political leaders and peoples."[102] At work here is a basic claim about human nature and, in particular, the social nature of persons. Todd Whitmore has pointed out the centrality of this concept within Catholic

97. International Theological Commission, *Memory and Reconciliation*, 2.1.

98. Ibid.

99. Ibid., 2.2

100. Bergen, *Ecclesial Repentance*, 220.

101. International Theological Commission, *Memory and Reconciliation*, 6.3

102. Ibid.

social doctrine. This tradition replaces the modern "presumption in favor of individual autonomy" with a robust sense of "interdependence" that is growing and "intensifying" as the world becomes globalized.[103] In the interdependent model, "even salvation is social," and thus while individual merit and guilt are still operative, "the formation of a social unit," to use the words of the Second Vatican Council, becomes the key moral task facing the human community.[104]

Bergen notes that a robust sense of communal responsibility is also central to political theory more generally. He quotes Elazar Barkan and Alexander Karn, who argue that "the individual is, to a significant degree, folded into the communities and groups with which she/he identifies and, further, that group members have a responsibility for the actions of others who identify (or have identified) themselves in the same way."[105] Bergen also cites the German philosopher Karl Jaspers, who proposed, in the wake of the Holocaust, a fourfold scheme by which to assess guilt. *Criminal guilt* applies to individuals who have directly violated laws or moral norms. *Political guilt* refers to those in authority who set policy allowing the evil and also to members of the community who actively or passively allowed such a climate. Two other categories are subjective: *moral guilt*, which can only be discerned in the conscience of persons facing up to their own role, and *metaphysical guilt*, which Jaspers applies to all human beings who together failed to stop the evil.[106] These categories can help illuminate a middle ground between a politics that collapses individual moral agency into categories of social sin and a politics that refuses to move beyond legal judgments to establish wider responsibility for harmful actions. In particular, the concepts driving Jaspers' categories of political and metaphysical guilt will form the basis for my proposal to introduce penitential solidarity as a response to the moral isolation experienced by soldiers coming to grips with the ethical dimensions of their participation in war.

The second challenge is rooted in my comprehensive definition of penance as practices through which persons lament, take responsibility for, and *seek to repair the wounds* that are caused by sin. Given these elements, the Jubilee gestures seem more precisely to be displays of repentance than acts of penance proper. On this topic, the MR text again deepens the

103. Whitmore, "Catholic Social Teaching," 61.

104. Ibid., 60, See *Gaudium et spes*, 32, and *Lumen gentium* 9.

105. Bergen, *Ecclesial Repentance*, 265–66.

106. Ibid., 263–64. See Jaspers, *Question of German Guilt*, 31–36.

principle at work. First, the ITC notes that the move from communal repentance to penance is part of a single process. In reference to the Day of Pardon confessions, "it is necessary to underscore that the one addressed by any request for forgiveness is God," which is also why MR follows the Vatican in not using the word *apology* to describe the gestures.[107] Yet this does not exclude the centrality of victims; rather, it highlights the role of divine agency in directing the repentant community to the wounds of victims. God's mercy enables what MR describes as the move from gestures of repentance to "gestures of reparation" that "*must* be connected to the recognition of a responsibility."[108] Especially in the case of centuries-old sins, that reparation "may assume a symbolic-prophetic character," but the ITC affirms that for the church, deep reparation of any kind flows from genuine repentance before God, in which "taking responsibility for past wrongs is a kind of sharing in the mystery of Christ, crucified and risen," whose divine, repairing love opens the way for the transformation of all victims and all perpetrators.[109] In this way, repentance is properly an element of penance insofar as its expressions of lament and responsibility initiate the work of reparation.

Bergen affirms that there is something irreducibly theological in ecclesial repentance—performed in a church whose very existence is based on Christ's forgiving response to wrongdoing, a narrative not at the core of most political entities—but he also collects a diverse array of scholars promoting the *political* repentance expressed in collective apologies. The voices assembled echo his point that such apologies are "speech-acts" that are more than words and promote social repair in specific ways.[110] Trudy Govier is invoked to show how apologies can put a community "on public record" and effect "a shift in attitudes."[111] Repentance also helps shift power dynamics toward victims since, as Martha Minow notes, "An apology is not a soliloquy."[112] In this way, repentance on behalf of a group introduces new voices to the conversation that constitutes the group's narrative. Even if some in the group do not support an apology or repentance—and this scenario is quite common—the perspectives of victims must be dealt with,

107. International Theological Commission, *Memory and Reconciliation*, 6.2.

108. Ibid.

109. Ibid.

110. Bergen, *Ecclesial Repentance*, 279.

111. Ibid., 279–80

112. In ibid., 280.

even if the result is a disturbing axiom like the one that arose in post-dictatorship Chile: "Truth doesn't bring the dead back to life . . . but it brings them out of silence."[113] Moreover, political philosopher Janna Thompson helps Bergen make the point that, since reparation will always fall short of returning to victims what was lost, apologies "should be understood as forward-looking" expressions about "what constitutes a present relationship of respect and power."[114] I would add to this defense of the political value of collective repentance that such acts also help uphold the moral norms that are the crucial undergirding for new relationships of respect. Put in the terms of Philpott's paradigm, collective apologies help "defeat the standing victory of injustice," which is a primary and crucial restoration of the political order.[115] He also notes secondary restorations, such as increased interpersonal trust and decreased risk for cycles of revenge.

For all of these reasons, then, communal repentance is not only beneficial in ecclesial settings but, furthermore, has broad political applicability to promote concrete and deep social repair. This claim will be the basis for my proposal that we adopt the model of repentance in response to recent American wars. Applying the logic proposed by the ITC, expressions of repentance can help *evoke* a commitment to repair. While some postwar models insist on the justice of reparations up front, as a kind of precondition to reconciling expressions, the Christian tradition—and my definition of penance—suggests, rather, that the proper starting point for social repair is lament. Emmanuel Katongole and Chris Rice argue that lament is a forgotten practice in many societies, including the U.S. What they call "the discipline of lament" may not ostensibly present action plans or political strategies, but it is a way to see clearly our communal brokenness and to approach together "the path toward being raised into something new."[116] My particular proposal will be for American political leaders and citizens to cultivate practices of lament in solidarity with a particular group: U.S. soldiers returning from war in Iraq or Afghanistan. The merit of such a proposal will depend not only on my preceding theological and political justification, but on demonstrating that the practice would serve the needs of soldiers themselves, especially those confronting a painful past of combat and trauma. Resources for analyzing precisely this need can be found by deepening what John Paul II and the ITC call "the purification of memory."

113. See Philpott, *Just and Unjust Peace*, 205–6.

114. Bergen, *Ecclesial Repentance*, 280–81.

115. See Philpott, *Just and Unjust Peace*, 200–205.

116. Katongole and Rice, *Reconciling All Things*, 198.

Indeed, the third challenge I want to raise at the end of this chapter is exactly how addressing *the past* relates to constructing a *new future*. This question was raised often in the wake of John Paul's Jubilee gestures, with many wondering how "digging up old wounds" was helpful as the church headed into a new millennium. But the question is also relevant today, for shared examination of recent events, like two costly wars, that may be just as tempting to move beyond. Thus, I will now address the question, how does "purification of memory" relate to social repair? As MR makes clear, "purification of memory" does not signal some attempt to deny or erase the past. Rather, the ITC emphasizes that it means "eliminating from personal and collective conscience all forms of resentment or violence left by the inheritance of the past."[117] In this way, it is not a forgetting, but rather a different kind of remembering, a "new evaluation of the past."[118] We can note here how much development has occurred in the life of the church, from the call in Vatican II for Muslims and Christians "to *forget* the past and to work sincerely for mutual understanding"[119] to the aforementioned offer of the Polish bishops to the Germans that "in spite of it all . . . let us try to forget!" A key element in that development is an understanding of the way in which individual and communal acts of remembering are a key basis for conscience formation.[120] Moreover, John Paul eventually makes the case in the final book he published, *Memory and Identity*, that remembering constitutes the very identity of the church: grounded in the sacred and collective memory of Scripture; embodied in Mary, who gives the church a "maternal memory" as she "treasured all these things in her heart" (Luke 2:51); and enacted in the Eucharist by which Christ instructs us, "Do this in memory of me" (Luke 22:19).[121]

Theologically, the act of remembering also has soteriological and eschatological implications. On this point, Bergen again points to important resources. The first builds on the patristic formula of St. Gregory Nazianzen about the salvific meaning of the incarnation of Christ on our behalf: "what is not assumed is not saved." Analogously, Lionel Chircop argues that "what is forgotten cannot be healed"—and moreover can become "the source of greater evil."[122] The insight here recalls the "theology of wounds" offered

---

117. International Theological Commission, *Memory and Reconciliation*, 5.1

118. Ibid., 6.1

119. *Nostra Aetate*, 3.

120. See Bergen, *Ecclesial Repentance*, 188.

121. John Paul II, *Memory and Identity*, 165–201.

122. In Bergen, *Ecclesial Repentance*, 188.

by Robert Schreiter, which emphasizes that the wounds of the risen Christ do not disappear but are transformed into marks displaying his *identity* as Jesus, the one whom the disciples know.[123] In a similar way, only in remembering a traumatic past do we allow those wounds to be healed and incorporated into the ongoing story of our identity as individuals and peoples. Of course, this highlights the moral importance of providing a safe space in which memories can be "purified," that is, placed in the context of healing and "an evaluation of the past" that is not dominated by "resentment and violence."[124]

Another resource, highlighting the eschatological dimensions of memory, comes from Miroslav Volf. He notes the limits to reconciliation in life before death, and that it is precisely the fullness of this process that is promised in the resurrection—an event as social as it is individual. Eternal life is, thus, the coming to fruition of "God's gift to the transformed self, enjoying reconciled relationships."[125] This will not necessarily mean holding on to painful memories forever, since Volf argues that "truthful memory does not have to be indelible memory."[126] Similarly, Bergen describes "the possibility that a truthful memory can be released, even recede in memory, because its truth remains embodied in reconciled relationships."[127] Thus, for victims of traumatic crimes, the actions of perpetrators not only do not have the final say on the memory of the event, but the memory itself may fade. This hope, for Volf, does not come quickly: victims cannot be forced into a paradigm of reconciliation. And it does not come cheaply: only in light of an eschatological gift of new life from God can this process come to fruition. Bergen concludes that "in a sense, memory is like a ladder which can be kicked away once the summit is reached, but it is crucial that the ladder not be kicked away too soon, or by the wrong person."[128] In light of God's plan for a future of full reconciliation, where relationships between victims and perpetrators cannot be escaped forever, the proper response therefore is neither forgetting nor gripping tightly, but holding memories open—sometimes quite slowly—to the possibility of transformation.

---

123. See Schreiter, *The Ministry of Reconciliation*.

124. International Theological Commission, *Memory and Reconciliation*, 5.1, 6.1.

125. Volf, *End of Memory*, 147.

126. Ibid., 64.

127. Bergen, *Ecclesial Repentance*, 191.

128. Ibid.

The principle that remembering the past is essential in God's construction of a repaired future is one that, like the others in this chapter, has clear implications for politics. One does not have to be a theologian to quote the famous line of Faulkner that "the past is not dead, it is not even past." Even legal and political philosopher Jeremy Waldron, who is skeptical of broad approaches that place historical injustices of the past into a paradigm of penance and reparation, appreciates the social value of communal remembering. Its importance emerges in the face of false narratives about the identities of people and their enemies:

> In the face of all this, only the deliberate enterprise of recollection, coupled with the most determined sense that there is a difference between what happened and what we would like to think happened, can sustain the moral and cultural reality of self and community.[129]

Nowhere is the difference between the way a people remember an event and what actually happened more prominent than in the case of war. This problematic difference is heightened when a community upholds one narrative of the war while returning soldiers often remember another. For this reason, my final chapter will suggest the need for acts of remembering—and, more precisely, the kind of acts described as "purification of memory"—as a penitential response to war.

In this chapter, I have traced in detail the deployment of gestures of repentance by John Paul II during the Jubilee Year. I noted the way in which his approach bore fruit in consequent acts of repentance and movements toward reconciliation by myriad other communities, including the G7 acting to cancel significant portions of the debt of poor countries. I also noted the ways in which a more robust commitment to penance would have helped heal wounds in response to the clergy sexual abuse crisis, a crisis that still marks the landscape of U.S. Catholicism. Lastly, I attempted to deepen in three ways the concept of penance on display in the gestures of John Paul II: its inescapably communal dimension, its intrinsic connection to reparation, and its relationship to the project of "purification of memory." Given this context, I am now ready to propose, in my concluding chapters, a substantive proposal to put communal penance at the service of concrete situations in need of social repair.

---

129. Waldron, "Superseding Historical Injustice," 6.

5

Applying the Politics of Penance:
Criminal Justice Reform

IN THE INTRODUCTORY CHAPTER, I laid out the social relevance of penance, defined as practices through which persons lament, take responsibility for, and seek to repair the wounds that are caused by sin. I then suggested that the value in my proposal would consist in the ability of the ethic to address the *wideness* of situations needing repair and to do so with a *depth* that actually is able to bring specific solutions to specific cases. I will now turn to this task.

In offering this religiously rooted, politically minded resource, I am guided by the theology of engagement that I outlined in my introductory chapter. Such engagement, I argued, is an expression of what Pope John Paul II called the "ordering of temporal affairs according to the plan of God."[1] This does not mean ecclesial control of the social arena, but it does invite men and women with public roles to consider insights from Christian tradition. Moreover, the call to engagement highlights the need to work within the context of "rooted reason," to use Philpott's term for rational arguments with deep resonances in both religion and politics. Finally, and perhaps most importantly, this political engagement works best when it stokes the moral imagination within a society. In this way, a consistent theme of my project is that Christ's repairing power is intended not only for the church but also for a wider world in need of new ways to fight injustice. N. T. Wright's claim that "the new creation launched in Jesus is good news for *all* people at *every* level" points to possibilities for "a better,

---

1. John Paul II, *Christifidelis laici*, 15. See *Gaudium et spes*, 43.

wiser, and fairer world."[2] My argument is that the path of penance lays open this repairing power, offering an underexplored resource for politics. But, as stated, the value of this ethic as a political resource needs to be explicated in political terms. And to that task I now turn.

The Crisis of Mass Incarceration

In the summer of 2013, the Judiciary Committee of the U.S. House of Representatives held the inaugural hearing of its newly created, bipartisan Over-criminalization Task Force. The five Republicans and five Democrats received testimony from experts, ranging from the president of the National Association of Criminal Defense Attorneys to the criminal justice chair of the American Bar Association to the legal director of the conservative Heritage Foundation think tank. All agreed that there is a deep problem. In opening remarks at the hearing, task force ranking member Rep. Bobby Scott summarized the crisis:

> In the last 30 years, we have gone from an average daily jail and prison incarceration level of about 500,000 to over 2 million, with an average incarceration rate of over 750 per 100,000 residents (male and female), a rate about seven times the international average.[3]

The statistics for persons of color are even more dire. Scott referenced a 2013 study by the Pew Research Center on the States, which reported that 4.3 percent of all black men, 1.8 percent of Latino men, and .7 percent of white men are incarcerated—rates that have roughly tripled for all three groups in the last fifty years.[4] In a separate study, Pew reports that prison spending has increased by more than 600 percent in the last twenty-five years, from around $10 billion to more than $60 billion per year, "and yet recidivism rates have barely changed."[5] For the world's leader in incarceration, the numbers simply are not adding up to a defensible or rational criminal justice policy, which is why Congress and an increasingly broad cross-section of American society are noting the scope of the problem.

2. Wright, *Scripture and the Authority of God*, 192–93.

3. U.S. House Committee on the Judiciary, "Over-criminalization," 3.

4. Drake, "Incarceration Gap," Graph 1.

5. Pew Charitable Trusts, "Public Safety, Public Spending," iv–v.

In fact, some elements of action have taken shape. Since 2010, the overall prison population within states has declined, though this change is not mirrored in federal prisons (where populations are increasing, but at a less rapid rate than previously).[6] One factor driving the moves to reduce incarceration is budgetary constraints, as prisons are notoriously expensive to operate. But, according to Adam Gelb of Pew, another key is a "growing awareness that there are research-based alternatives that cost less than prison and work better to reduce recidivism."[7] A good example of the need for progress comes from California. In May 2011, the United States Supreme Court, in a 5–4 ruling, upheld a lower court decision ordering the governor to reduce the prison population by a third. In order to meet this demand, the state is looking toward programs such as probation incentives, which send some of the money saved on incarceration to programs that successfully reduce recidivism and promote rehabilitation. Still, mass incarceration poses not only a technical but a moral challenge, and to this end I offer the penitential ethic. As I stated in the opening paragraph of this book, it is not common for policymakers or social activists to turn to a concept like penance for solutions, but the principles I have illustrated throughout my work can yield some practical paths toward the repair of criminal justice.

Lament: Making Masked Injustice Visible

Emmanuel Katongole argues that lament is "a first language in a broken world" and often the only means by which those without social power can acquire a voice.[8] In the biblical tradition, lament is a powerful form of speech for the marginalized, on full display in the Psalms, among the prophets, and in the Passion of Jesus, with his lament over Jerusalem (Matt 23:37) and his cry from the cross (Matt 27:46). But Katongole also notes that after Jesus' birth, "which is the birth of a new social reality," we hear "a voice from Ramah, of loud lamentation, Rachel weeping for her children" (Matt 2:18). In this way, the social pain—which anticipated the arrival of Christ and which draws our attention today—so often comes "from Ramah, a marginal place, outside of the center."[9] Lament thus involves a kind of "relocation," a change of perspective from which a challenge is seen, not

---

6. Pew Charitable Trusts, "U.S. Prison Population Drops for Third Year," para. 1.

7. Ibid., para. 3.

8. Katongole and Rice, *Reconciling All Things*, 77.

9. Katonogle, "Born of Lament," part 4.

only for those who receive a lament but for those who offer it.[10] Their cry is the first attempt to live into a new society in which their situation matters. In terms of the penitential ethic, lament recalls the example of Pope John Paul II, whose Jubilee gestures unleashed a cascade of efforts in which communities sought to resolve intractable social issues in a spirit of self-critical dialogue. In this way, Katongole concludes that practices of lament are illuminating disruptions to entrenched narratives, helping us *unlearn* our innocence, *unlearn* our distance from the margins, and *unlearn* our confidence that our group has all the solutions.[11] What, then, does lament look like in the midst of the present crisis in criminal justice?

One good example is Michelle Alexander's 2010 book, *The New Jim Crow: Mass Incarceration in the Age of Colorblindness.* She sets the bleak statistics concerning the incarceration of black men against a larger canvass of economic and political marginalization. For example, she analyzes the economic changes concomitant with the rise of black incarceration. In the 1970s, a massive exodus of manufacturing jobs from urban centers began as a result of corporations' preference for factories in countries with lower labor costs. Moreover, the good jobs that were emerging in technology sectors gave preference to workers with high levels of education. Indeed, the text that came to epitomize urban life in this era was William Julius Wilson's book *When Work Disappears.*[12] Alexander does not minimize the dramatic rise in the illicit drug economy that ensued—leaving behind "unspeakable devastation and suffering," especially when crack cocaine came to inner cities in the 1980s.[13] But she also points out some facts that disrupt the narrative that the main culprit was internal to black culture: "In 1954, black and white youth unemployment rates were equal. . . . By 1984, however, the black unemployment rate had quadrupled."[14] And although minorities had always been sent to jail at higher rates than whites, "until the mid-1980s, the criminal justice system was marginal to communities of color and [quoting a study of the data] 'the penal system was not a dominant presence in disadvantaged neighborhoods.'"[15]

---

10. See Katongole and Rice, *Reconciling All Things,* 75–94.

11. See ibid.

12. See Alexander, *New Jim Crow,* 50.

13. Ibid., 51.

14. Ibid., 218

15. Ibid., 188

The epicenter of her lament is the mid-1980s, when what she calls "The Lockdown" began. America did have a choice. Other countries facing a similar challenge of rising crime rates "chose the path of drug treatment, prevention, and education or economic investment in crime-ridden communities."[16] Yet in the War on Drugs, though there were exhortations to "Just Say No," the weapon of choice was incarceration—and the face of it became the gangbanging black crack addict (along with the "crack whores" who became the face of social spending reduction plans). New laws facilitated quick prosecution (even waiving many rules on how evidence is obtained) and enacted mandatory minimum sentences, "including far more severe punishment for distribution of crack—associated with blacks—than powder cocaine, associated with whites."[17] All this, says Alexander, was the perfect storm for the New Jim Crow:

> Black men found themselves unnecessary to the American economy and demonized by mainstream society. No longer needed to pick cotton in the fields or labor in the factories, lower-class black men were hauled off to prison in droves. . . . Decades later, curious onlookers in the grips of denial would wonder aloud, "Where have all the black men gone?"[18]

Even if one does not concur in full with Alexander's assessment of the history, or her attribution of this situation to "a well-orchestrated political campaign,"[19] this is a lament worth hearing at a time when "young black men are more likely to go to prison than to college."[20]

In my view, then, this becomes the first suggestion of the penitential ethic: a conversation, deep and wide, among whites and persons of color about the role of incarceration in our communities. This would not be a series of "chats" but instead a comprehensive process, perhaps even authorized by Congress through its Over-criminalization Task Force and led by trained facilitators who guide a structured process leading to final reports and recommendations for a plan of action. Following the vision of justice as right relationship that I have defended in this book, the truth is that current crime policy may in fact be *incapable* of justice in the presence of a deep relational gap between races. Indeed, in this gap appears what

16. Ibid., 51.

17. Ibid.

18. Ibid., 219.

19. Ibid.

20. Ibid., 190.

Frederick Douglass called "the heavy and cruel hand" that has been laid upon black Americans: "Our white countrymen do not know us. They are strangers to our character, ignorant of our capacity, oblivious to our history and progress, and are misinformed as to the principles and ideas that control and guide us as a people."[21] For more white people to enter into relationship with fellow citizens who are black would be beneficial to politics and criminal justice policy, but such conversations would not be just about blacks. Rather, the story of mass incarceration is also about the role of white people—not just those governing, but all whites. And raising the question of complicity could evoke lament from new social locations.

Alex Mikulich, Laurie Cassidy, and Margaret Pfeil have addressed this question in their 2013 book, *The Scandal of White Complicity in US Hyperincarceration: A Nonviolent Spirituality of White Resistance*. Pfeil's constructive project concludes the book and brings into sharp focus the penitential skills needed for the conversation I propose. Pfeil asks us to consider our own role in the crisis, challenging facile assurances that socially destructive violence is what criminals unleash, not us. In response, through the discipline of spiritual self-awareness, "little by little, one comes face to face with all the manifold impulses toward the violence of dominative power within one's own heart and way of being."[22] This discipline is not easy, and its cultivation has been central to the monastic tradition. As I noted in chapter 2, the Desert Fathers and Mothers practiced *exagoreusis*, the opening of one's heart, and the Irish enshrined this self-examination as "confessio" with a trusted guide with whom to engage in "healing dialogue." Here we begin to see the deep resource that the monks of Ireland provide us, helping to cultivate lament within ourselves and appreciating the lament of others, both of which are key skills in order to establish a healing dialogue on the crisis of mass incarceration. And before dismissing these practices as fit for a monastery but not for the rough-and-tumble of our own day, we do well to remember that the Irish society encountered by the monks was as violent and crime-ridden as any in the ancient world—and penitential self-examination was the tool they wielded in successfully transforming it.

Ultimately, this first practice of the penitential ethic offers the possibility of a shared lament that can open paths of social repair. In this way, black Catholic theologian Shawn Copeland notes that lament is not a vague state

---

21. Frederick Douglass, "Statement to the National Colored Convention, 1853," in ibid., 140.

22. Mikulich et al., *Scandal of White Complicity*, 156.

of sadness but is "a practice of justice" that "protests, pushes against that calculus of power," which accepts marginalization.[23] Even more specifically, Bryan Massingale argues that white people will not engage a crisis in the black community "solely or even principally through intellectual responses." Rather, "lament makes visible the masked injustice hidden beneath the deep rationalizations of social life."[24] In the civil rights movement, powerful laments—such as Emmett Till's grieving mother deciding to hold an open-casket public funeral for her butchered fourteen-year-old—changed the course of history. It is impossible to chart the possibilities for lament in this crisis, but the practice will help deepen and widen the conversation. As we saw in early Irish society, criminal justice does not emerge from specific verdicts and punishments, but from *the kind of community* in which these are practiced and *the openness of all members* of that community to cultivating a capacity for repentance. Thus, promoting a healing dialogue about the crisis of mass incarceration is essential to becoming the kind of community that can be trusted with responsibility for criminal justice.

Responsibility: Medicinal Punishment

In his book on the role of repentance in civic life, Solomon Schimmel asks a central question of this case study: "Are there ways in which our criminal justice system can encourage a criminal to repent?"[25] Schimmel begins his affirmative answer to the question by noting the obvious etymological significance of the fact that "criminals are sent to *penitent*-iaries, suggesting that they are expected to become penitent and repent for their crimes during their stay in prison."[26] While noting the religious connotation of the term, he defends the idea that there is such a thing as "civic, moral, or secular repentance . . . which do not depend on theological assumptions or religious commitments."[27] The public importance of penitence hinges on the meaning that we as a society give to punishment. Presently, it seems we are not quite sure why we punish. Christopher Glazek, for example, suggests that prison sentences in America function largely to physically move

---

23. Copeland, "Political Theology as Interruptive," 181.

24. Massingale, *Racial Justice and the Catholic Church*, 110.

25. Schimmel, *Wounds Not Healed by Time*, 183.

26. Ibid.

27. Ibid., 190.

sites of crimes from cities to incarceration facilities.[28] He reports that when the Justice Department began last decade calculating sexual assaults inside correctional facilities, it became clear that "prison rape accounted for the majority of all rapes committed in the US."[29] Using this as just one example, he argues that we punish criminals to "shift" their violence, and then call it reduction.

A more common punitive rationale is retribution, and the principle driving this model is desert. That is, hardship is imposed on an offender simply because their crime deserves to be punished. If it is not, according to Immanuel Kant's famous dictum about not executing the last remaining murderer on an island, "the people can be regarded as collaborators in this public violation of justice."[30] I will have more to say on the retributive rationale, but first I wish to focus on a related option that has more, though not total, resonance with the penitential tradition.

Philosopher Nicholas Wolterstorff, following Joel Feinberg and others, proposes what he calls a theory of "reprobative punishment" in which legal authorities, on behalf of a society, order an offender to "hard treatment" in response to the breach of morality and justice.[31] Wolterstorff distinguishes this view from retributive theories because the penalty imposed is a "life-good" for the offender, rather than a payback that balances the crime through a tit-for-tat mechanism. This view has some affinity with the "expressivist" theory of punishment endorsed by Daniel Philpott. Philpott sees punishment as a key means by which society communicates censure and rejects "the standing victory of the wrongdoer's injustice."[32] This does involve hardship, including physical removal to a prison for certain crimes, which Philpott explains using an analogy to penance itself:

> Just as an injustice involves an action, not mere words, so, too, does the message of punishment. Only imposed deprivation can communicate commensurately the gravity of a crime. If a perpetrator should choose to accept a punishment, then the hardship becomes his participation in the defeat of the evil he committed— much like a penance.[33]

28. See Glazek, "Raise the Crime Rate."

29. Ibid., section 2.

30. Kant, *Metaphysics of Morals*, 142, in Philpott, *Just and Unjust Peace*, 217.

31. Wolterstorff, *Justice in Love*, 193–97.

32. Philpott, *Just and Unjust Peace*, 219.

33. Ibid., 223.

An interesting and significant question raised by this understanding of punishment is whether hard treatment, or "imposed deprivation," is *necessarily* a part of punishment as penance. Both Wolterstorff and Philpott decry the conditions in many contemporary prisons, making clear that hard treatment can never involve the violation of human rights. Moreover, Philpott in particular emphasizes the role of community-based programs for less serious crimes and argues that even prison itself can be a restorative experience in the cases of more serious crimes. But he insists on the element of hardship in these cases, and ties it directly to penance. Is this position tenable, and does it have a role in a penitential ethic that addresses the problem of crime?

The concept of hard treatment does have an impressive provenance in secular and religious thought. And, as Wolterstorff and Philpott attest, it is not always associated with retributivism or a payback mechanism. Simone Weil argued that punishment must inculcate the "thirst for good," but that "sometimes it may be necessary to inflict harm in order to stimulate this thirst" until the soul "awakens with the surprised cry, 'why am I being hurt?'"[34] A related rationale is that the hardship suffered serves to remind the perpetrator of the victim's experience, thus eroding a perpetrator's putative attempt at superiority over them. In this way, as philosopher Jean Hampton notes, how a society punishes reveals the value that it places on victims. Consider, she says, the reality of longer prison sentences for those convicted of killing a white person rather than a person of color. Such an unjust fact reveals not just the racism of our system but also, for Hampton, the natural connection between punishment and victim value. She notes that hardship or pain is not the *only* tool to communicate a recalibration of value between offender and victim—and here Hampton does endorse a retributive balancing mechanism—but that hardship is well suited to establish the essence of punishment: submission. For her, "punishment is an experience designed to 'humble the will' of the person who committed the wrongdoing" with the result that he sees "that the law (and not he himself) is 'boss.'"[35]

Though on terms distinct from the above rationales, hardship does have a place in the penitential ethic I propose. Consider the Irish monks. Many of the penances involved physical hardship: long periods on spartan food allotments, significant experiences of manual labor, and exile from

---

34. Weil, *Anthology*, 74–75.

35. Murphy and Hampton, *Forgiveness and Mercy*, 126–27.

the comforts of home to unknown communities. Moreover, in this context, penance was understood conceptually and existentially as a punishment. And, indeed, the wrongdoer was expected by the community to submit themselves to a new "boss," a monk who was understood also as a dispenser of public justice. And yet in the penitential principles gleaned from the monks, hardship is only one element in a constellation of practices that includes rebuilding self-worth, forgiveness, and "publicly and solemnly being reintegrated with society."[36] They promoted "medicamenta penitentiae," medicinal punishment, which I described in chapter 2. Second, as noted above, hardship can only be considered a moral good in the context of a political society able to dispense it justly. This, too, was a key insight of the monastic communities of Ireland. Thus, hardship, in my view, cannot be a *sine qua non* of the punitive rationale. While no system is perfect, the already-cited litany of abuses and racial domination exhibited by the American system continue to raise the question of whether we are morally capable of dispensing hardship in a trustworthy way.

Thus, while in theory prison can be a place in which the soul is awakened, the experience inside American prisons often reveals the opposite result. As Glazek notes, "as much as a physical space, prisons denote an ethical space," but in the U.S. it is "more precisely, a space where ordinary ethics are suspended." He continues,

> Far from embodying the model of Bentham/Foucault's *panopticon*—that is, one of total surveillance—America's prisons are its blind spots, places where complaints cannot be heard and abuses cannot be seen. . . . As far as the outside world is concerned, every American prison functions as a black site.[37]

Interestingly, liberal advocates like Glazek have an ally in contemporary Catholic social teaching. In her work "Just Punishment? A Virtue Ethics Approach to Prison Reform in the United States," moral theologian Kathryn Getek highlights, in particular, a 1978 statement from the U.S. Catholic Bishops' Conference titled "A Community Response to Crime." In this text, the bishops issue a sweeping indictment of American prisons, which "communicate a message of hopelessness and of community anger devoid of concern" while denying the moral agency of prisoners' "individual decision-making and responsibility."[38] Getek adds that "according to

36. Weil, *Anthology*, 75.

37. Glazek, "Raise the Crime Rate," 3.

38. USCCB, "Community Response to Crime," in Getek, "Just Punishment?," 74.

the statement, even the small proportion of inmates of serious crime who require structured settings would be better in community-based confinement" that avoids a "problematic separateness from the community."[39]

Seen in light of my earlier description of the late 1970s as a time of rising joblessness and violent crime in urban centers, the bishops' statement represents an early "canary in the coal mine" of hyper-incarceration strategies. More recently, the USCCB issued, in 2000, *Responsibility, Rehabilitation, and Restoration: A Catholic Perspective on Crime and Criminal Justice*.[40] In this text, the bishops acknowledge that society "should punish offenders and, when necessary, imprison them," but that "incarceration should be about more than punishment."[41] In particular, they call for a move of "public resources away from building more and more prisons and toward better and more effective programs aimed at crime prevention, rehabilitation, education efforts, substance abuse treatment, and programs of probation, parole, and reintegration."[42] As Getek notes, a key move in this text, "repeated several times," is "the assertion that punishment must never be for its own sake."[43] This is a potentially confusing claim, since even those who favor a retributive view would argue that punishment serves an end beyond pain infliction, such as re-establishing the dignity of victims. Moreover, the "never for its own sake" could raise problematic utilitarian applications that undermine a value intrinsic to punishment: the communication of moral censure. But the basic point of the bishops is clear: "Our society seems to prefer punishment to rehabilitation and retribution to restoration thereby indicating a failure to recognize prisoners as human beings."[44] On the whole, this critique is consistent with the penitential principles embodied by the Irish monks, who were deeply committed to the moral agency of perpetrators in the performance of their penance.

Theologian Andrew Skotnicki argues that the bishops miss the way in which retributive and restorative justifications are mutually reinforcing, "twin principles" that, by necessity, impose hardship. He sees the correct insight on most vivid display in a 1955 address of Pope Pius XII, "Crime and Punishment," which likens the retributive-restorative relationship to

39. Getek, "Just Punishment?," 74.

40. USCCB, *Responsibility, Rehabilitation, and Restoration*, sec. 6.

41. Ibid., sec. 7.

42. Ibid.

43. Getek, "Just Punishment?," 76.

44. USCCB, *Responsibility, Rehabilitation, and Restoration*, sec. 2.

the painful action of a surgeon intending to bring health to a diseased patient.[45] He also suggests that the bishops fail to appreciate the role of prison. Interestingly, Skotnicki likens the early church order of penitents to the contemporary conceptualization of prison: "a class of excluded offenders, under communal supervision, in an assigned place, for a period of time, and bearing, as did Scriptural penitents in sackcloth, a special corporeal symbol."[46] Skotnicki admits that prisons—both ecclesiastical ones historically and American ones currently—have been rife with abuse, but he resists the conclusion that their just use cannot be re-established. What drives his claim is that "the confinement process itself, with its methodological elements of ritual shaming, temporal exclusion, isolation, prayer, and silence, is an effective catalyst for moral renewal."[47] Skotnicki also roots the defense of prison in monastic culture, such as "the house of penitents" described by St. John Climacus as "a mile from the great monastery."[48] Yet he cannot rely heavily on the wisdom of the Irish monks since, as I have shown, their model was not so much an endorsement of incarceration, exclusion, and isolation as it was an inscription into a fresh set of interpersonal relationships. This did sometimes involve exile to a new community, but that community was not comprised solely of other offenders. Moreover, some of the crucial work of penance was done precisely in physical and moral proximity to the victims and the society harmed by the offense. Still, the penitential ethic I am proposing can incorporate two of Skotnicki's key insights.

First, as he notes, many secular justifications for prison focus on incapacitation and deterrence, reasons that give punishment (and prisoners) only instrumental value. The penitential tradition seeks a deeper rationale that takes seriously the nature of punishment as a moral act. Second, he rightly identifies a precise question that prison is designed to answer: "How to create contrition among those who do not feel contrite?"[49] This is a crucial question for a penitential ethic, especially given that contrition is so clearly "a necessary element in the development of penance."[50] And the fact that American prisons often produce not contrition but alienation does not

45. Pius XII, "Crime and Punishment," in Skotnicki, "Foundations Once Destroyed," 800.

46. Skotnicki, "Foundations Once Destroyed," 802.

47. Ibid., 805.

48. Ibid., 806

49. Inid., 810.

50. Ibid.

itself provide an answer. Thus, the pressing task is to locate a theory and praxis that offers an alternative to the present system while retaining the authentic aims of punishment. Such a theory is offered in the medicinal punishment of the Irish monks, which I will continue to illustrate below. This approach does not, in my view, mean fleeing entirely from the concept of imposed hardship, or even prison, but rather presenting a paradigm that envelops it more clearly within the scope of restoration. This would involve creating institutions and communities designed to achieve what Philpott calls "the repair of persons, relationships, and communities" affected by crime, including repair to "the wounded soul of the perpetrator."[51] I will now outline the way in which a particular set of practices—increasingly known as restorative justice—can refine and improve the performance of this kind of punishment-as-penance.

Reparation: Restoring Justice

Philpott points out that, as a criminal-justice reform movement in Western societies, restorative justice has "existed—at least in explicit form—only for some three decades."[52] This explicit form he defines as "practical alternatives to the sequence of trial, sentencing, and imprisonment" that "involve gathering all of the relevant parties to a crime and seeking a solution that promotes restoration for as many of them as possible," especially through the use of mediators between victims and offenders.[53] For Philpott, the strength of restorative justice emerges when we see a particular crime not merely as a "violation of law" but as "a rupture of right relationship," that is, an injustice that calls for repair to a wide range of material and moral wounds.[54] Restorative paradigms have long existed within indigenous societies, a point that helps strengthen their potential for public use in an "overlapping consensus" of more public recourse to this model. The principles that drive the restorative model are also on clear display in the Christian penitential tradition.

The most illustrative example from the Irish monks came in response to the most corrosive of crimes—murder. There, the punishment of exile and imposition of the *pietatis obsequia* or *Goire* (Irish for "the

51. Philpott, *Just and Unjust Peace*, 219, 230.

52. Ibid., 65.

53. Ibid.

54. Ibid., 66.

warming")—by which the perpetrator would work for the economic good of his victim's kin—was aimed not only at restitution but at "thawing" thick layers of tribal violence through interpersonal encounters and economic interdependence. And this Irish penance involved real hardship. All of the proceeds from work were saved, since no money could be spent on meat or wine, and only slowly would the perpetrator move from exile to reintegration, from servitude to equality. The difference between the Irish model and our own, then, is not so much the extent of hardship—as if our system is tough on crime and theirs was not—but rather the social context and goals within which that hardship is faced. The clarification of social context to include the whole community, including victims, and the specification of social repair as the goal are, in fact, the key elements of the vision of Howard Zehr, one of the leading articulators of restorative justice in the United States.

Zehr's 1990 text, *Changing Lenses*, has helped conceptualize many practical initiatives, especially experiments with VORP (Victim Offender Reconciliation Program), which was first attempted in the U.S. by Mennonites in Elkhart, Indiana, in 1978. Though his presentation of restorative justice is comprehensive, I will focus here on the way it construes the moral repair of victims. I do so because of the similarity of Zehr's vision to that of the Irish monks, and also because prevailing criminal-justice processes so often leave out victims. Zehr identifies several common needs of those harmed by crime. Restitution is crucial, but he argues that, in fact, victims "usually rate other needs more highly," such as "the need for answers, for information. Why me?"[55] Some of these answers may lead to the need for confrontation, a safe arena in which to express *to* offenders their pain and anger. Western courts sometimes provide this, but do not meet victims' related need of "a sense of control or involvement in the resolution of their own cases," which provides the kind of empowerment necessary to restore dignity.[56] Zehr addresses other crucial needs, such as safety and communal condemnation of the wrong done to them, all of which lead to his claim that what victims most need is "an experience of justice."[57] He admits that "justice cannot guarantee or force reconciliation, but it ought to provide opportunities for such reconciliation to occur."[58]

55. Zehr, *Changing Lenses*, sec. 2.
56. Ibid.
57. Ibid.
58. Zehr, in Getek, "Just Punishment?," 82.

Zehr's paradigm, therefore, is participatory; the community's response to crime is not merely dispensed in a verdict, but enacted by those most affected: "Justice may be a state of affairs, but it is also an experience. Justice must be experienced as real. Victims are not usually content to be assured that things are being taken care of."[59] This model has clear implications for incarceration strategies. While it might seem that more victim involvement would mean harsher and longer sentences, Zehr uses the research of Russell Immarigeon to suggest that "victims are often open to nonincarcerative, reparative sentences—more frequently, in fact, than the public."[60] Zehr's insights bear striking resemblance to those of the Irish penitentials. As I noted in the case of murder, and as with offenses of every other kind, the needs of the victim were always at the fore of punitive measures. This included attention to full restitution for what happened in the past, as well as a view toward ongoing needs in the future. Moreover, the monks perceived a difficult but ineluctable truth that Zehr seems also to intuit: after crime, the lives of offenders and victims simply are intertwined. This reality can be difficult and even appalling, and the force of it may often prevent full healing. But the fact of this dysfunctional union cannot be undone, and if justice is to be in any sense comprehensive for the victim—or a social force to prevent cycles of revenge—it must take account of and seek to repair the relationship.

If Zehr provides key justifications to understand the role of victims in this paradigm, then Australian scholar John Braithwaite will serve as an excellent resource to understand the way in which restorative justice proposes to best respond to offenders. Interestingly, he was first influenced by Asian policing practices and by Western parenting styles, both of which confront wrongs with, among other things, "moral reasoning."[61] From there, he encountered the "substantial body of empirical evidence" that "the justice system will do better when it facilitates moral reasoning by families over what to do about a crime as an alternative to punishment by the state."[62] For this reason, he favors VORP models that involve nuclear and even extended family members, and not only of victims but of offenders too. From the standpoint of moral repair for the offender, the reason for this model is that it "structures shame into the conference," since "it is not the shame of

59. Zehr, *Changing Lenses*, sec. 2.

60. Ibid. See Immarigeon, "Broad Support for Alternative Sentencing," 1–4.

61. Braithwaite, "Restorative Justice," 1.

62. Ibid.

police or judges or newspapers that is most liable to get through to us; it is shame in the eyes of those we respect and trust."[63] This dynamic is part of Braithwaite's comprehensive "reintegrative shaming theory." As opposed to "outcast shaming," which leads easily to alienation (and which is on display today in the American prison system), reintegrative shaming allows multiple levels of society to communicate moral censure to one who has done wrong, but within a context of hope.

For Braithwaite, several key features of the restorative justice "conference" process protect the goals of reintegrative shaming. One is procedural justice. Though courts and trials operate within the constraints of more rules and safeguards, in fact, "conferences are structurally fairer because of who participates and who controls the discourse."[64] Here, process matters. Using a study on recidivism in domestic violence cases, as well as broader research in Tom Tyler's 1990 book, *Why People Obey the Law*, Braithwaite notes that offenders "were more likely to comply with the law when they saw themselves as treated fairly by the criminal justice system."[65] In this data, even arrestees' experiences of whether police had "taken the time to listen to their side of the story" were predictors of recidivism.[66] This insight is particularly important within a police and judicial system that are, as I have noted, so deeply distrusted in the black community. In fact, Braithwaite points out that greater police accountability to the community is one of the features of the conference process, which can include officers involved in the arrest. Moreover, he notes that "offenders are more likely to say they trusted the police after going through a conference with them than after going through a court case with them."[67] All of these are reasons why Braithwaite prefers family/community conferences to one-to-one mediation of victim and offender.

Models like VORP/conferencing can thus provide what Zehr called "an *experience* of justice," but they also are more open to the kind of penitential, contrition-evoking emotions that I have upheld as socially beneficial. In fact, on this score, Braithwaite points out that courtroom models may produce the problem of "unacknowledged" or "bypassed" shame. The basic idea is that when all attention and resources are focused on producing "a

63. Ibid.
64. Ibid., 2.
65. Ibid.
66. Ibid.
67. Ibid., 8.

verdict" of innocence or avoiding the "outcast shaming" of prison, there is little structural incentive for contrition. He quotes David Moore's observation that in standard trials, appropriate shame is often suppressed and "hidden behind impersonal rhetoric about technical culpability."[68] Even when judges allow letters or testimony to ask for leniency in sentences, the most effective strategy is often to focus on how good the offender is in other areas of life, not how sorry they are about the wrong. In this way, the dominant model of events leading up to incarceration actually makes much harder the already daunting task that Skotnicki described as creating contrition among those who do not feel contrite. But, for Braithwaite, the danger is not simply that standard trials miss an opportunity to initiate contrition or reintegrative shaming, but that the unacknowledged shame will emerge in destructive ways, such as what he calls the "shame-rage spiral."[69] Thus, what is important about restorative justice processes in this regard is that "they create spaces where there is the time and the tolerance for shame to be acknowledged."[70]

The model that Braithwaite defends is remarkably similar to the approach of the Irish monks. They developed the penitentials precisely to guide the careful craft of inculcating contrition without removing hope for correction. Their model was explicit that only when the sinner can "beat his breast" and "through weeping and tears" come to contrition is it possible for the *medicamenta penitentiae*, medicine of penance, to bring health. What provided the hope, and the only context in which the penances made sense, was the "effective and healing dialogue" that took place between the sinner and his trusted companion, who tended to the repair of both his body and his soul. Brathwaite's emphasis on the role of family and friends in the restorative justice process makes the same point about creating the conditions in which reintegrative shaming will flourish. In this way, restorative justice corresponds to the need for a specifically *penitential* approach to crime and punishment. If we want offenders to lament, take responsibility for, and seek to repair the wounds they have caused, then this model deserves more attention. Of course, we need to be careful not to assume that "decarceration" equals restorative justice. Skotnicki fears that in the current milieu of a "management ideology," always seeking "low-cost forms of social control" such as "drug testing, electronic monitoring, and

68. Ibid., 4.
69. Ibid., 3.
70. Ibid.

intensive probation as surveillance mechanisms"—and these in the guise of "alternatives to prison"—the result could be that we simply "'downsize' the traditional prison in favor of creating virtual penal colonies in many poor urban neighborhoods."[71]

The answer to this specter, in my view, is attention to doing restorative justice right, and not under the rationale of cost-savings, nor with overreliance on the mechanisms of social control just noted. But I wish also to address Skotnicki's larger point, that we ought not to abandon hope for prison as the institution in which penance can be best done. Indeed, if one assumes that society will continue to have incarceration as an element of criminal justice, then we ought to consider one final aspect of restorative justice. Can it be practiced well *inside* of prisons? I believe that the answer is yes. While the model is best performed within the community, several features of it—and, interestingly, features quite relevant to penitential principles—are possible within the prison walls. Solomon Schimmel, for instance, draws specifically on Jewish and Christian construals of penance to suggest that prisons "provide opportunities for inmates to volunteer their services to others in need."[72] Such service might focus on the needs of other prisoners or even on work that earns money to be used in restitution to victims. This practice corresponds precisely to the idea of "fructum penitentiae," the fruit of penance, which the Irish monks employed to tie penance to restitution, and it also corresponds to key tenets of restorative justice. A further practice noted by Daniel Van Ness of Prison Fellowship, a Christian group that, in fact, operates some "virtuous prisons" according to the restorative justice model, involves prisoners meeting with their victims, a process that has worked when there is "a lengthy preparation process designed to ensure that the victims and prisoners are ready for such a meeting and that it will not result in secondary victimization."[73] Other practices, such as the appointment of "godparents" for prisoners in cases where their family has disowned them, also help navigate the penitential and restorative path of inculcating contrition without removing hope for correction.[74]

A final and crucial dimension of the penitential ethic involves restoration back into the community. One of the most beautiful aspects of religious tradition is the attention given to the community's welcome of a sinner who

71. Skotnicki, "Foundations Once Destroyed," 815–16.

72. Schimmel, *Wounds Not Healed by Time*, 194

73. Van Ness, "Restorative Justice in Prisons" 3–5.

74. Ibid.

has done penance. Jesus invokes a triad of parables—the lost sheep, the lost coin, and the prodigal son—to emphasize that "there will be more joy in heaven over one sinner who repents than ninety-nine righteous who have no need of repentance" (Luke 15:7). In the early church, as I illustrated, the rite of welcome would occur at the end of Lent and be celebrated by the penitent being embraced and then rejoining the community around the eucharistic table. The return of sinners looks quite different in the United States. Alexander refers to the "black box" that so many African-American men must check on post-prison employment applications, which often seals their fate as permanently poor, second-class citizens.[75] Of course, in some states, many released prisoners are second-class citizens literally, denied the right to vote as the result of a felony conviction. In a host of other crushing ways—from the financial debts with court offices to social exile in the community—prisoners continue to be punished after their release.

Against the claim that, for many black men, prison has become a "badge of honor" without stigma on re-entering society, Alexander cites Donald Braman's ethnographic study, *Doing Time on the Outside*, in Washington DC, "where three out of every four young black men can expect to spend some time behind bars."[76] Braman concludes that in fact "they are not shameless; they feel the stigma" that accompanies incarceration.[77] The most prominent response to life after incarceration, argues Alexander, is not "shamelessness" but "severe isolation, distrust and alienation."[78] The damage related to these three emotions—isolation, distrust, and alienation—is precisely what the penitential ethic aims to prevent. In fact, the entire program of penances proposed by the Irish monks was designed to cultivate community, trust, and commitment, a "cure by contraries" approach to the perils of reintegration. And the monks employed a kind of subsidiarity to achieve this repair, preserving the individual moral agency by which penitents would personally reintegrate into just relationships but also preserving the solidarity by which the community would support and receive them. Today, justice in the wake of crime cannot be the sole domain of the state: that model is failing.

In contrast, I have proposed that penance—practices through which persons lament, take responsibility for, and seek to repair the wounds that

75. Alexander, *New Jim Crow*, 151–54.

76. Ibid., 164.

77. Braman, *Doing Time on the Outside*, 219.

78. Alexander, *New Jim Crow*, 165.

are caused by sin—be reintroduced to the prevailing lexicon of crime and punishment in the United States today. More specifically, I have shown that my penitential ethic illuminates the keys for this task: listening for lament through shared public dialogue, promoting responsibility through medicinal punishment, and repairing wounds through the employment of restorative justice.

6

Applying the Politics of Penance: Truth and Reconciliation

FROM 1980 TO 2000, an internal armed conflict claimed the lives of seventy thousand Peruvians, with the majority of the victims being poor, indigenous campesinos living in villages in the Andes Mountains. The war erupted in response to the insurgency of a Communist terror group known as *Sendero Luminoso*, or Shining Path. The strategy of *Sendero* was to enter the villages of the Andes to build an army that would then be capable of overthrowing the government in Lima. They would use denunciations of Peru's blatant inequality and racism toward Andeans for motivation, but they also employed threats and targeted killings. As a result, the movement spread, and in 1982 the government responded with its armed forces. The military used many of the same tactics as *Sendero*, "bailando a su musica" (dancing to their music, i.e., playing the same game of terror).[1] Carlos Sanchez, a marine in Peru's armed forces sent in 1983 to Ayacucho, described the torture tactics: "We would hang suspects by a rope from a helicopter, where all could see them, then we would cut the rope."[2] Even more common was the "disappearance" of persons. Soldiers would enter villages and round up suspects, torture them for information, kill them, and not disclose the remains of their bodies.

One important part of the story of "los desaparecidos," the disappeared, is that many were totally innocent. In the military's war, they did not distinguish *Senderistas* from legitimate social activists. Consider, for example, the case of Doris Caqui de Capcha:

1. Onis et al., *State of Fear*.
2. Ibid.

> I am the mother of four children. My husband's name was Teofilo
> Rimac Capcha. He was a great union leader and a teacher. On 23
> June 1986, the military raided my house and grabbed my husband.
> They took him to the military base; I never saw him again.[3]

One of the questions that is addressed by the penitential ethic is, what does the government of Peru owe to victim-survivors like Doris Caqui de Capcha? A critical point relevant to this question is that this violence was not a case of random "bad apples" in the military. It was *political violence* against citizens, planned and authorized by the very government responsible for protecting them. And in Peru, this political violence was carried out as political leaders declared national emergencies, giving the military permission to act with impunity. As a result, though *Sendero* was responsible for approximately forty thousand killings, most of the remaining thirty thousand were perpetrated by the country's armed forces.[4] The turning point in the war came in early 1992. The decisive blow came not from the military but from the laborious work of detective Benedicto Jimenez, who uncovered the house where *Sendero* founder Abimael Guzmán was staying. With their organization decapitated, the structure of *Sendero* began to collapse, and by 2000 the conflict had effectively been ended.

The era of openly repressive government ended, too, and one of the first acts of transition was the establishment of a truth commission, later to be recast as a truth and reconciliation commission—Comisión de la Verdad y Reconciliación (CVR). The work of the CVR, which began in June 2001 and concluded in August 2003, was impressive. It received seventeen thousand personal testimonies, with interviews and hearings held in 530 districts and 137 provinces in every region of Peru.[5] Despite many obstacles, including financial ones, the CVR pursued a comprehensive agenda, which included the investigation of human rights violations as well as the recommendation of an Integral Plan of Reparations (PIR) for victim-survivors. One key decision of the CVR was to reject the possibility of forms of amnesty in exchange for the testimony of perpetrators of the violence, a strategic move that was adopted in other countries (most notably South Africa). As a result, the overwhelming majority of the testimony was from victim-survivors. The CVR did, in fact, receive private, "off

---

3 Peru Support Group (PSG), *Findings of Peru's Truth and Reconciliation Commission*, 25.

4. Ibid., 6.

5. Ibid., 11.

the record," and anonymous testimony from some military officers.[6] The information gleaned in these sessions was key to the remarkably thorough investigations of the CVR, but did not substantively inscribe state agents into the reconciliation process.

Moreover, many of these actors were openly hostile to the Final Report of the CVR. While polls suggested that a majority of Peruvians had a positive impression of the commission, several prominent generals attacked the report, arguing that it besmirched the military and played into the hands of enemies of the state.[7] One of the most prominent critics was Cardinal Juan Luis Cipriani of Lima. At a Mass held just after the release of the CVR report, in the presence of Peruvian president Alejandro Toledo, Cipriani announced, "I do not accept it because it is not true."[8] The Peruvian Bishops' Conference itself issued a positive response to the report, but the public opposition of Cipriani has compromised the extent to which the goals of reconciliation have penetrated the Catholic Church. And, in turn, this has compromised its ability to penetrate the larger culture with reconciling tools. Overall, while the CVR itself was a model of comprehensive and inclusive processes, key aspects of implementation stand out as failures. The International Center for Transitional Justice (ICTJ) concluded in 2013, on the tenth anniversary of the Final Report, that in particular "the trials of people accused of grave crimes are proceeding at a slow pace, the needs of victims do not receive adequate attention, and the demands of the families of thousands of disappeared people are met with inaction and indifference."[9]

In this application of the penitential ethic, I will offer some modest insights into ways that the concept and practice of penance might help construct positive action on the twin challenges of punishment and reparations referenced by the ICTJ. Specifically, I will draw heavily on Thomistic principles from chapter 3 in order to suggest that a key goal must be the motivation of former perpetrators—who are still in control of wide swaths of political power in Peru—to participate in social repair. My argument will unfold once again by way of the three practices at the heart of penance.

---

6. Ibid., 13.

7. Ibid., 42.

8. Forero, "Peru Truth Commission Stirs Up a Hornet's Nest," 5.

9. International Center for Transitional Justice, "Ten Years after Peru's Truth Commission."

Lament: Understanding the Cries from the Andes

I have noted that, while the CVR highlighted the anguish of so many Andeans who suffered the brunt of the violence, it was not successful in displaying the laments of state agents who participated in killing raids in the Andes. For this kind of broad and effective lament, we must turn to those Andean villages themselves. Theidon, the anthropologist who has spent more than two decades living and working in Ayacucho, the "cradle" of the violence, reports fascinating rituals of lament that occurred in the wake of the "sasachakuy tiempo," a hybrid Quechua and Spanish term for "the difficult years." She concludes, "There is a lament in the communities with which I have worked: 'Jesucristo, look what we have done among brothers.'"[10] Significantly, the prevalence of this kind of self-indicting anguish gave rise to contrition and the confession of wrongdoing. In one of the most striking contrasts from the experience of the CVR, she describes the rituals of the "arrepentidos," repentant ones, who emerged in Andean villages after the violence. These *campesinos* knew of the national strategies but were often skeptical, pointing out to Theidon that they had "propias practicas," their own practices, and "nuestra justicia interna [our internal justice]" to deal with the past.[11] The *arrepentidos* were former *Sendero* insurgents, villagers who had been swept up by the call to revolution or had been coerced into the movement. In either scenario, they had killed many of their "projimos," neighbors. During the war itself, villages had agreed that such militants should be killed or given over to soldiers to be killed. Yet, as violence subsided, the traditional "emphasis on rehabilitation rather than execution" led to "rituals to deal with those 'liminal people' who wanted to deliver themselves to a human community."[12]

The first element of the ritual with the *arrepentidos* was confession—and their confessions were not anonymous but public. This feature was, in part, the result of a kind of amnesty by which the community decided *not* to deliver the *arrepentidos* into the hands of the state—though they were punished, as we will see. Second, those who were repentant never presented themselves to the villages alone but always with their family. As one village elder, Mama Marcelina, told Theidon, "When they arrived as families, we had more trust. They could be *runakuna* [people] again."[13] Third, after

10. Theidon, "Justice in Transition," 435–36.

11. Theidon, *Intimate Enemies*, 240.

12. Theidon, "Justice in Transition," 446.

13. Ibid., 448.

their public confession, they were confronted by the villagers. "Are you going to stop being like that?" Mama Marcelina recalled asking. "We asked them over and over again."[14] Theidon argues that this interpersonal and discursive element, especially the confession, is central to justice. She cites Peter Brooks' point that Roman Catholic sacramental practice must not be undervalued as a resource: "confession of wrongdoing is . . . fundamental to morality because it constitutes a verbal act of self-recognition as wrongdoer and hence provides the basis of rehabilitation."[15] The rituals involving *arrepentidos* in Andean villages were aimed at a kind of interpersonal lament—by both victims and perpetrators, displaying grief and reinforcing contrition—and point to the justice of reconciliation in a way that the national dialogue was unable to achieve.

Pfeil cautions that the work of the CVR not be dismissed in this regard since it "represents the annunciation rather than the culmination of a process of reconciliation."[16] This annunciation, she further specifies, also took explicit account of the fact that "reconciliation needs to unfold on the interpersonal level" and that "nothing can substitute for the role of personal encounter in the process of healing and reconciliation."[17] Pfeil also quotes the CVR report in its assessment that "true repentance" would lead "institutions or persons directly involved in acts of violence to publicly acknowledge their guilt before society" in order to "create the new conditions of solidarity that national reconciliation requires."[18] As we have seen, and as Pfeil acknowledges, this vision has not been achieved, but perhaps the experience of rituals for the *arrepentidos* in Andean villages provides a kind of empirical verification of the CVR ideal. That is to say, what the CVR articulated, the Andeans embodied. To put the matter in terms of the penitential ethic, the villages were able to engage in practices that inculcated the *virtue* of penance. As I noted in chapter 3, Aquinas insisted that penance is not only a sacrament but a virtue, one that is both a gift of God and a human practice. This idea squares with the Andean experience of the *arrepentidos*, especially since Theidon reports that the villagers were

14. Ibid., 446.

15. Ibid., 448. See Brooks, *Troubling Confessions*, 2.

16. Pfeil, "Social Sin: Social Reconciliation?," 176.

17. Ibid.

18. Ibid., 173. See CVR, I, "Introducción," 38 and IX.1, "Fundamentos de la Reconciliación," 14.

guided in part by "sacramental principles" and an explicit awareness of the reconciling will of God.[19]

In this way, Andean practice points to an insight of the penitential ethic: with displays of lament can come a breakthrough that is generative of a commitment to social repair. For Aquinas, this creative breakthrough requires a community that is open to and formed for the virtue of penance, and is also related to the way in which the community chooses to punish the penitent. That is, when punishments correspond to the virtue of penance, they are more able to be evocative of the kind of contrition and commitment to social repair that is so desired. The villages had a long-standing commitment—both religiously and rationally—to this approach, upholding the "norms of the community via public rituals steeped in confessional reasoning."[20] And thus, on the question of how to construe taking responsibility for wrongs, we see another clear contrast between national processes and the "propias practicas" of the Andeans.

Responsibility: Punishment-as-Penance

Theidon reports that consistent among many Andean communities were "long-standing patterns of administering retributive and restorative justice in these villages."[21] In the context of the postwar presence of many former *Senderistas* in their midst, this meant tough punitive measures. But it also meant keeping as the goal "to convert the Senderistas into people again."[22] In this way, Theidon affirms the basic instinct of the penitential ethic, which construes penance not as an alternative to punishment but rather as a restorative expression of it. Indeed, echoing Skotnicki's analysis of a Catholic approach to justice in the previous case study, Theidon concludes,

> I do not believe that restorative and retributive justice are distinct or opposing forms of justice. . . . Rather, I find that retributive emotions are very common and not intrinsically "Western" and that some form of punishment may be conducive both to the reincorporation of the perpetrator as well as to restoring social relations among transgressors and those they have wronged.[23]

19. Theidon, "Justice in Transition," 449.

20. Theidon, *Intimate Enemies*, 240.

21. Theidon, "Justice in Transition," 445.

22. Ibid.

23. Theidon, *Intimate Enemies*, 418 n. 33.

The ways in which Andean villages pursued this dual retributive-restorative goal in punishing former killers is illuminating. When the *arrepentidos* came forward (along with their families) to the village, the type of punishment they faced meant the difference between life and death. If they were handed over to soldiers, they would be forced to dig a hole, then shot and buried in it.[24] For this reason, the *arrepentidos* begged the villagers not to tell the soldiers—"oh how they pleaded, sobbing," reported Mama Marcelina.[25] And the villagers complied, administering a form of punishment deeply resonant with the concept of penance I have proposed.

After a public confession and intense questioning from the community, the *arrepentidos* would be watched, "watched for where they might go, night and day."[26] The image here suggests a kind of social incarceration, though there was no actual prison and the *arrepentidos* were living with their families. Once the village was convinced that repentance was possible, the former killers would face the corporal punishment of public scourging with *chicotes*, whips of braided leather: "Whipping them, they were received here," reported one villager.[27] The emphasis was not so much on the physical suffering incurred, but on the kind of shaming invoked in the previous case study, using the work of John Braithwaite. And this intense period of shame only began the process of reintegration: "confessing, atoning, sobbing, apologizing, begging, promising—sincerity would depend on both words and action."[28]

The next step in punishing *arrepentidos* in these Andean communities also strikes a chord with the penitential practices I have detailed. Having been accepted by the community as penitents seeking to be "musaq runakuna," new people, the *arrepentidos* were put to work.[29] Theidon was surprised at the way in which this manual labor program was constructed. One day she found in the *Actas Comunales* (record of community meetings) for a village in Ayacucho references to giving "the abandoned lands without owners" to the arrepentidos.[30] This meant, she discovered, that some of the very lands formerly owned by persons killed in the violence,

24. Theidon, "Justice in Transition," 447.

25. Ibid

26. Ibid.

27. Ibid.

28. Theidon, *Intimate Enemies*, 241.

29. Theidon, "Justice in Transition," 451.

30. Ibid.

or those who had fled, would be given to those who shared responsibility for inflicting the violence. In this particular village, the land chosen was near the burial holes of former insurgents killed by police—a reminder of the alternative fate they avoided but could face again. The expectation was that the *arrepentidos* would work the land for their personal and communal benefit. As Mama Marcelina put it, "So they could build homes they gave them land, and land to work. They are still working, and like us they are eating. They became *runa masinchik*—people we work with, people like us."[31] Theidon does not romanticize this process, nor does she claim that it was universally employed. In one community, which tied would-be penitents to a large stone personified as "Judge Rock" as they were interrogated, some with *mayor delito*, "greater guilt or crime," were killed—though this was during the war itself.[32] Moreover, it is not clear if the problem here was too much blood on their hands or too little repentance in their hearts, since Theidon reports that even "cabezas," leaders of *Sendero*, were given the chance to repent and receive "an arrangement."[33]

Perhaps more relevant than its universality in practice is the fact that the repentance rituals were not universally accepted. Consider this transcript Theidon shares of her conversation with a widow whose husband had been murdered by *Senderistas*, some of whom perhaps became *arrepentidos*:

> "Look at them," she said, "they have houses, land, animals. Me? What do I have?" She angrily shook her head.
>
> "What do you think of this?" I asked, already sensing her response.
>
> "We remind them sometimes that if it weren't for us, they'd be dead. They're only alive because people here allowed it." She spit her tired wad of coca on the ground in disgust.[34]

Still, Theidon concludes that "working on communal land was a form of atonement," and an effective one, in which the *arrepentidos* would be inscribed into a system of "reciprocity, in social networks."[35] The rationale here matches exactly the *pietatis obsequia* practice of the Irish monks, by which they imposed on murderers manual labor for their own preservation

31. Ibid., 452.

32. Theidon, *Intimate Enemies*, 245.

33. Ibid.

34. Ibid., 248.

35. Theidon, "Justice in Transition," 452.

and the good of their victim's family, with the goal that economic interdependence would curb cycles of revenge. And, as with the Irish penances, this Andean practice was "remarkably successful in stopping lethal violence at the communal level."[36] Moreover, the program of penance was construed explicitly as a form of *punishment*. Though it benefited the perpetrators, it also was a way of marking them, setting them apart as clearly beholden to the community. It does not, she insists, indicate a kind of forgive-and-forget dismissal of their crimes. The perpetrators did receive a kind of pardon, but "my power or authority to pardon you does not mean we are equals. The *arrepentidos* would be reminded of this."[37] The process thus appealed to the retributive emotions of victimized communities while also helping restore the perpetrators. In this way, it provides a clear example of what punishment-as-penance looks like.

The CVR made clear from the outset that the form of justice it required in the wake of political violence began with judicial prosecution of perpetrators. As noted, they rejected any idea of offering levels of amnesty for public testimony, and in fact they suggested that such a trade would signify "the abandonment of justice."[38] The CVR argued that "the first step toward reconciliation can only be made if those who perpetrate crimes against humanity . . . assume the responsibility, appearing before the Courts and paying their debt to society."[39] Indeed, as the report notes, the state can successfully prosecute, evidenced by the many *Senderistas* sentenced to prison. And yet prosecutions of state agents—the forty-two named in the report or the thousands of others involved in the deaths of thirty thousand Peruvians—have had only limited success. Part of the reason is that prior laws gave state agents immunity from prosecution, especially Fujimori's 1995 measure. But this law was overturned—by Peru's Congress and then, in 2001, by a verdict of the Inter-American Court of Human Rights[40]—and still prosecutions are rare. Jo-Marie Burt, a specialist in judicial response to human rights abuses in Peru, estimates that between 2005 and 2010, there were fifty-eight convictions, compared with eighty-five acquittals, and of course the vast majority of cases never even went to trial.[41] Peru

36. Theidon, "Intimate Enemies," in Pouligny et al., *After Mass Crime*, 118.

37. Theidon, *Intimate Enemies*, 248.

38. PSG, *Findings of Peru's Truth and Reconciliation Commission*, 34

39. Ibid.

40. This came in the famous Barrios Altos case before the IACHR.

41. See Burt, "Análisis de las sentencias."

did make global history in 2009, when Fujimori was convicted for his role in orchestrating massacres during the war. Burt notes that this was "the first time that a democratically elected head of state in Latin America has been found guilty of committing crimes against humanity" and "the first time [in the world] that a former president has been extradited to his home country to face charges for such crimes."[42] Still, taken in full context of the death-dealing war, prosecution for political violence has largely failed to achieve accountability for those with enough access to state power to avoid punishment.

Thus, the difference between the villages and the CVR is not that the former rejected the punishment of hard treatment. As one Andean woman commented in reference to the abuses and crimes the military committed during the war, "Let the generals spend at least a few months in prison so they understand what it means to suffer."[43] This comment is telling, because the "few months" construal differs from the desires of national human rights leaders in ways that may be more realistic—and which certainly do not see prison as the primary means of punishing these serious crimes. Moreover, as Theidon confirms, the village model prioritizes personal, dialogical justice over a more institutional, judicial model. She heard this "common refrain" vis-à-vis the CVR: "So *los doctors* from Lima think they can come here and tell us to reconcile? If the soldiers want to reconcile with us, then let them come here and apologize and repent for what they did."[44] Given the creative forms of punishment to which the villages were open, perhaps that is precisely what should have happened—and still could happen. State agents who are the focus of lengthy, costly, and probably futile efforts to bring them to justice before a judge might be allowed as an alternative to face the people.

In any case, what is clear is that that the standard prosecution model often on display in the wake of political violence is not the only, or most effective, punishment paradigm. Rather, as shown in the Andean communities, another vision emerges. This vision was not applicable only to "lesser" crimes—remember that this region was the *most ravaged* by the violence of Peru's internal armed conflict, and the *arrepentidos* had often killed the fathers, brothers, and sons of those who then imposed penance on them. Moreover, unlike the dominant model, Andean punishment is

42. Burt, "Fujimori on Trial."

43. Theidon, "Justice in Transition," 454.

44. Ibid.

quite expressive of religious tradition and the agency of God. It is not that they use religion as a "resource"—Theidon notes that "villagers did not speak *about* religion but rather spoke *with* religion"—but that their practice embodied the traditional goals of confession, "the curing of souls and re-affirmation of community."[45] By taking seriously what Philpott calls "the wounded soul of the perpetrator," these villages seek to be instruments of God's healing purposes in the world. For them, that means a concept of penance-as-punishment, by which the community affirms the norms of its members even as it seeks the possibility that, with God's grace, a perpetrator might be counted among them once again.

Reparation: Not Getting Even but Getting Equal

So far, I have not emphasized one of the key features of postwar justice: reparations for victim-survivors. This practice is, of course, evident in the practices of the Andean villagers, with *arrepentidos* working land for their personal and the common good. But recall my point at the outset, that much of the violence during the war was political violence in its most proper sense, carried out by agents of the state. Thus, in addition to—and perhaps, from victims' perspectives, even more important than—prosecutions, justice demands an official redress of wounds. In particular, as I have argued, such reparation is a *sine qua non* of restorative justice. This point was recognized by the CVR. One of their key recommendations was the establishment of an Integral Plan of Reparations (PIR), which would "compensate for the violation of human rights, the losses and damages incurred—social, moral and material."[46] These measures were to take the form of symbolic reparations (gestures, monuments), individual reparations to victims (economic compensation as well as access to health and educational redress), and collective reparations (to communities, though the CVR was clear that this was not to be confused with the necessary work to resolve widespread "problems of poverty, exclusion and inequality").[47] But if the final report was clear in setting out the goals of restorative justice in the wake of the war, then once again the political reality has come up far short.

In June 2013, reparations expert Cristián Correa released a report for ICTJ that analyzed the state of the question ten years after the CVR

---

45. Ibid., 449.

46. PSG, *Findings of Peru's Truth and Reconciliation Commission*, 37.

47. Ibid., 37–38.

report. Correa noted that most of the recommendations were passed into law in 2005 and that Peru created a high-level commission and Reparations Council to carry out the plan and create a registry of victims. At the end of 2012, the registry included 160,429 individuals, 77,072 of whom were deemed eligible for compensation, and 7,678 communities eligible for collective reparations.[48] Attention to this latter groups has, at times, produced results, according to Correa, since the law prescribes that the communities themselves should choose and direct the projects, with most of them aimed at economic recovery, sanitation, electrification, or the preservation of cultural heritage. Still, only 1,946 communities have received these reparations, and the administration of them (externally and internally) has tended to exclude women from equal participation.[49] Moreover, it has not always been clear to communities that the projects were, in fact, forms of reparation, and sometimes the needs addressed were ones that the government had an obligation to address anyway, such as roads and schools. Peru began collective reparations in 2007 and total spending neared the $100 million USD mark by the end of 2013.

Individual reparations only began in 2011. Intense debates surrounded the question of how much compensation would be paid, and to whom. The 2005 reparations law, as well as a 2013 follow-up, specified that no former insurgents would be eligible for the registry of victims or for reparations, though Correa rightly insists that this contradicts the inalienability of human rights and has opened the door for suspicion and discrimination.[50] In addition, budgetary pressures impinged on discussions of the amount of compensation. In 2011, a thousand victims received a one-time payment of 10,000 soles ($3,700 USD), but, after public outcry and a change in administration, a new decision was reached by the high-level commission that the amount allocated to every victim—those who were killed, disappeared, disabled, or raped—would be 36,000 soles ($13,500).[51] In cases of death or disappearance, half of this amount would go to a surviving spouse, and the rest to children and parents.[52] This decision, though less than what victims groups desired, was promising because the total projected spending was $1.2 billion USD over ten years. Unfortunately, the same administration

48. Correa, "Reparations in Peru," 10.

49. Ibid., 12–13.

50. Ibid., 6.

51. Ibid., 16.

52. Ibid., 16–17.

(of Ollanta Humala) that showed promise has now reverted back to the earlier compensation levels and failed to meet targets for the number of victims compensated. By the end of 2012, a total of 17,652 individuals had received compensation from the state of Peru in the amount of $36.7 million USD.[53] This represents less than a quarter of all those already registered as beneficiaries of reparations. And Correa expects that "the current trend of providing isolated measures will continue."[54]

One interesting barometer of Peru's lack of progress on reparations is evident in decisions and orders of the Inter-American Court of Human Rights. The Court has repeatedly ordered Peru to pay reparations, and even though Peru, under Paniagua in 2001, had signed an agreement with the Inter-American Commission of Human Rights to commit to investigations and reparations, "the state has generally failed to comply with these terms."[55] Of course, part of the challenge in Peru is a lack of financial resources and budgetary pressures. In this regard, as I noted briefly in chapter 3, Pablo de Greiff suggests that the IAHCR rulings may have been unrealistic and even unhelpful. By his estimate, the basic compensation the Court expected for each victim was $150,000 USD, a figure that, if applied to all victims, would be larger than the national budget.[56] And, since many of these rulings came out in the exact same time period as the CVR work and report, de Greiff believes that such demanding figures eroded the government's buy-in to reparations. His assessment of the past squares with Pfeil's hope for the future of reparations in Peru. Compensation will fail "by the measure of strict justice," but "from a more restorative vision of justice," the question can shift from "what is due each party?" to "what needs to be mended?"[57] In this sense, reparations can represent "a communal and dialogical" task that "involves the whole society."[58] Yet, even by this more expansive and less financially costly standard, Peru is failing, especially since the voices of victims—those from the marginalized communities of the Andes, in particular—are so often absent in the halls of power.

The need for restorative justice is also indicated by an interesting conclusion drawn from the research of Lisa Laplante among those indigenous

53. Ibid., 19.
54. Ibid., 29.
55. Ibid., 27.
56. De Greiff, *Handbook of Reparations*, 456–57.
57. Pfeil, "Social Sin, Social Reconciliation?," 185.
58. Ibid.

communities. Working with Theidon, she interviewed victims who *had* shared their experience with the CVR but *have not* received reparations from the state. She concluded that "there is an implicit contract established in the giving and receiving of testimonies about a painful history of sustained political violence."[59] While some victims did make reference to the need for punishment, "everyone expressed the desire for restorative justice through reparations."[60] Moreover, this was not only an *ex post facto* desire, but "the absolute majority explicitly justified their participation with the hope of concrete redress from the government."[61] In this way, the testimonies of victim-survivors were not simply "gratuitous gestures" but connected to "expectations" about what would result from their revelation.[62] Consider the exasperation of Justiniana Huamán, a widow from Ayacucho:

> Oh, why should I remember all of that again? From the top of my head to the bottom of my feet, from the bottom of my feet to the top of my head—I've told what happened here so many times. And for what? Nothing ever changes.[63]

These are the words of one whose hope has been dashed. Telling their story often is, quite literally, all that victims have to offer in the search for "un poco de justicia," a bit of justice—a phrase that came from many of those interviewed by Laplante.[64] Thus, when combined with the original trauma, the lack of political reparation—even after sharing openly the pain of it— creates a second wound without doing anything to treat the first. Thus, what justice looks like to Justiniana might challenge the current paradigm in Peru.

Roman David and Susanne Choi, using research with victim-survivors, criticize what they call the "perpetrator-centered" approach that focuses on prosecutions as the first step in transitional justice. They found that victims are more interested in "getting equal" in socioeconomic terms than "getting even" through state judicial mechanisms. Their research has important implications, since they found that even the granting of amnesties can be accepted if a vigorous program of reparatory justice is enacted.

---

59. Laplante and Theidon, "Truth with Consequences," 231.

60. Ibid., 240.

61. Ibid.

62. Ibid.

63. Ibid., 229.

64. Ibid., 243

Moreover, the capacity of victim-survivors for reconciliation, even reconciliation with those who committed the crimes, is made possible "when victims hold social positions that are on a par with their perpetrators."[65] This tracks what Ernesto Verdeja, following Nancy Fraser, refers to as the importance of "status parity" in which victim-survivors are elevated in political, social, cultural, and economic arenas.[66] In Peru, those who work for the implementation of the CVR are clearly committed to this vision, and yet they seem unwilling to consider ways in which compromise on judicial prosecutions might generate buy-in on reparations—an option that could be an appealing alternative for both victims and perpetrators. As I noted in chapter 3, Aquinas himself saw the need to move beyond the inadequacy of the justice "of judges" in which "the discretion of the offender or of the person offended" is not taken into account.[67]

My reference to "buy-in" above is meant quite literally. While as a state Peru is certainly constrained financially in a way that impinges on reparations, many of those who were involved at high levels in political violence are not—and thus could be an important resource of reparative funds. And they should be: while the state must be held to account for violence done in its name by military or security agents, individuals, too, should be asked to settle moral and material accounts. Bartolomé de las Casas had precisely this insight, and he tried to leverage the financial largesse of the conquistadores for the work of social repair. Ultimately, his punitive strategy failed to motivate these wealthy purveyors of violence, but what about other approaches—particularly one that employs the Thomistic insight that sinners need to be capacitated through punishment that is full of mercy and hope for a new future? "Mercy for perpetrators" is not a slogan that will be attractive to many, though by "mercy" I do not mean turning a blind eye or coddling, but rather the goal of restoration and inclusion of their gifts in the rebuilding of society. And clearly, in Peru, some of these gifts are financial. If the central strategy were to carefully create relationships between military/political elites and Andean victim-survivors, perhaps fresh motivations for social repair would be generated.

I do not pretend to offer this as an easy solution to the present intransigence of those responsible for the political violence and marginalization of Andean peoples. But the present strategy is failing. And in this

65. David and Choi, "Getting Even or Getting Equal?," 188

66. Verdeja, "Normative Theory of Reparations," 449.

67. Aquinas, ST III 90.2

alternative approach, progress would not be measured by how successfully the state can prosecute and lock up these well-resourced perpetrators
(though this would remain part of the strategy), but rather more centrally,
by how successfully they buy in to the hope for a new Peru. This approach
would be more meaningful to victim-survivors—and remember, for Aquinas, the work of satisfaction must be done "according to the will of the
person offended."[68] Thus, even if it meant less suffering and more mercy for
perpetrators, this strategy would seek a key resource of restorative justice,
one articulated in Aquinas' maxim about the need for the "raising of the
spirits toward the realization of the arduous good."[69]

Theidon's report from Andean villages provides a basis for hope in
what she calls "the micropolitics of reconciliation."[70] She concludes sharply,

> My research with communities in Ayacucho prompts me to assert
> that "national reconciliation" is several steps behind the transi-
> tional justice that campesinos have elaborated and practiced in
> the face of the daily challenges of social life and governance at the
> local level where intimate enemies must live side by side.[71]

I will conclude by examining how this micropolitics reflects insights from
my main resources—especially Thomas Aquinas—and forms the basis for
a modest proposal by which the penitential ethic of social repair might help
Peru on the macro level to pursue more effectively the goal of reconciliation.

A step toward reconciliation is evident in the way that Andean villages illustrate the concept of "purification of memory" advanced by John
Paul II and described in chapter 4. That is, the Andeans are clear that when
an *arrepentido* is reintegrated to the community, "the moral stain disappears . . . but not the memory of it."[72] The people still "recordar, pero sin
rancor"—remember, but without bitterness.[73] This concept tracks John
Paul's insistence that healing can come to communal memory such that the
past is not erased but rather is overcome by the renewal of right relationship. On the national level, several prominent leaders have closed off the
possibility of healing memories, a sentiment captured by the testimony of
former President Alan García in a 2003 appearance before the CVR: "El

68. ST III 90.2
69. ST I-II 25.1.
70. Theidon, "Justice in Transtion," 455.
71. Ibid., 456.
72. Ibid., 453.
73. Ibid.

Perú will never forgive, will never forget, and will never pardon that which it has suffered and that which it has lived."[74] In some ways, García's sentiment—clearly directed at the evils of *Sendero Luminoso*—is mirrored by an exclusive focus on prosecuting the past as the only way to begin healing the memories of political violence. Of course, a pressing danger after war is the creation, often by the "victors," of false or sanitized memory—and the CVR's greatest achievement was to make this impossible. But the insight of John Paul II was that unless memories are healed, the actions of the perpetrators will have the final say about what is true of the society itself. In this way, as the International Theological Commission specified, the purification of memory does not change the past but rather undertakes a "new evaluation" of it.[75] What might this mean in Peru today? Could reconciliation be construed in ways in which the goal is not so much to confront or prosecute the past but to truthfully forge a new future in which it is possible to "recordar, pero sin rancor"?

This balance of historical memory and purified memory is not easy, but it points toward the urgent need for societies to create new horizons of possibility for community and justice. The ITC, in an earlier 1982 text on reconciliation, had emphasized that while these new horizons are an eschatological gift of God, they also reveal the deeply "anthropological" practice of penance and its power within human history.

> Wherever men convert themselves, do penance and confess guilt, they touch upon the deepest secret of the person . . . and by way of anticipation, man's hope is fulfilled. . . . Because penance in its general human and religious form anticipates in a fragmentary way what is given by Jesus Christ to those who believe, it may be designated as a "sacramentum legis naturae," a sacrament of the natural law.[76]

The final reference in this ITC passage is to an argument of Thomas Aquinas. Indeed, it is Aquinas who most clearly illustrates the need to generate new horizons of possibility in order for reparation to be possible.

In many ways, the two strategies of reconciliation in Peru—one national and one indigenous—correspond to the two approaches embodied by Bartolomé de las Casas and Thomas Aquinas, described in chapter 3.

---

74. Ibid., 454.

75. International Theological Commission, *Memory and Reconciliation*, 6.1

76. International Theological Commission, *Penance and Reconciliation*, A, II, 4. See Aquinas, *Commentary on the Sentences* IV, 22, q 2 a 3.

Like Las Casas, the CVR was intent to hold high the social suffering of victims and demand in justice that perpetrators be ready to take full responsibility before any hope of reconciliation could be realized. Aquinas and the Andean villages, on the other hand, seemed to understand that perpetrators would need some form of hope in order to generate the kind of motivation and commitment necessary to undertake the work of social repair. On a practical level, this raises again the question of whether I am proposing that amnesty be used in order to correct presently failing paradigms of national reconciliation. While not offering a technical response, I would echo here some key Thomistic insights, drawn from religious tradition but not—as Aquinas so clearly insists—at odds with natural justice. For example, Aquinas construes the sacramental pronouncement of absolution as precisely a form of amnesty. It is an amnesty that does not forego punishment—since for him the penance (satisfaction) is a restorative punishment—but that does allow the perpetrator to elude the full measure of indictment from God. Correlatively, the Andean villages, drawing, as Theidon notes, on "sacramental principles,"[77] offered a kind of amnesty by which the *arrepentidos* eluded the harsh hand of the military but through which they were inscribed into a robust program of repair. What does this strategy gain that is relevant to macro-efforts in Peru?

First, the kind of amnesty on offer by Aquinas and the villages might gain the buy-in to reparation that I have argued is so critically missing in Peru. I agree with many in the human rights community there that the forms of amnesty granted in 1995—and even briefly invoked in a short-lived 2010 law that would have nullified any trial more than three years old—are odious and promote impunity. But the Thomistic-Andean amnesties keep the perpetrator "on the hook" in productive and creative ways. I also find odious the appeal to repentance issued by Fujimori in 1992 when his *Ley de Arrepentimiento* offered lighter sentences to *Senderistas* who came forward and "named names." It is interesting that this law did motivate large numbers (6,630), but it also produced false accusations and human rights abuses.[78] By contrast, the sacramental-village amnesties focus on the confession of the agent and taking personal responsibility for the wrong. It is true that navigating a kind of amnesty-for-reparation scheme is complicated and may not effectively bring well-protected military and state agents to the table. But it is also true that at a certain point, judicial

77. Theidon, "Justice in Transition," 449.

78. Theidon, *Intimate Enemies*, 234.

prosecution for past crimes simply loses its social power. In his book *When Brute Force Fails*, Mark Kleiman follows eighteenth-century Italian jurist Cesare Beccaria in arguing that punishment must be "swift and certain."[79] These two aspects are far more important than severity, an insight embodied fully by the sacramental-village model in which the penances are immediate, even if not as harsh, as the judicial verdicts, which take years in courts, if they ever come at all.

Much more work needs to be done to consider the ways in which reconciliation in Peru might benefit from a more penitential approach, though there will be reasonable objections. Correa himself has commented to me that in terms of national policy, "I am not very optimistic of a repentance approach" because of the inevitable manipulations and the fact that "in my experience, genuine repentance is rare."[80] No doubt, the politics of penance are messy, but in one sense, the power of the Thomistic paradigm is that the contrition of the penitent need not be a finished product as they enter into the reparative work of satisfaction. That is, Aquinas insists that a reconciling power is unleashed by the process, deepening the original motivation and making it more genuine. To be sure, the sacrament will not "work" with one who simply "fakes contrition," but by this understanding of penance, the grace of God is able to work with a little to produce a lot. The Andean villagers seemed to understand this, as evidenced by the message of elder Don Elias to a communal assembly: "We must work together and reconcile among ourselves with the love of our Lord. In this way our Lord will bless us, *in double* He will give us His blessing."[81] On the national level, some examples of this process in other countries do exist, as Correa more optimistically reminded me. In Timor-Leste, for example, a Community Reconciliation Process (CRP) brought forward more than fifteen hundred penitent perpetrators who sought adjudication at the interpersonal level.[82] It is true that, for cases of killing, rape, and torture, a judicial process was mandated, but the CRPs did in fact deal with many serious crimes, and, in these cases, UN representative Piers Pigou concludes that it was the presence of relevant village actors that gave the process "gravitas."[83] No such coordinated national program has ever been tried in Peru.

79. See Kleiman, *When Brute Force Fails*.
80. Personal Interview, August 8, 2012.
81. Theidon, *Intimate Enemies*, 238.
82. Pigou, "The Community Reconciliation Process."
83. Ibid.

As I move to a closing suggestion, let me reiterate a point: the penitential ethic is not at odds with judicial prosecution nor in principle opposed to prison as a just punishment. But the ethic does reject the notion that these two practices exhaust the appropriate and possible forms of punishment. Indeed, it seems that by construing punishment in such strict and secular categories, the CVR was not only being unrealistic but perhaps missing the chance for some measure of accountability, restorative justice, and reconciliation. And it is this reluctance to employ religiously rooted practices that I wish to address in my final suggestion. The CVR in Peru, like so many others, did invoke religious tradition—even the concept of reconciliation itself—in its report, but as we have seen the main measures by which it construed justice all hinge on actions of the state. In contrast, the penitential model of the Andes was rooted in "sacramental principles" and structurally reliant on the grace of God.[84] Theidon even notes that the same verb, *se entregar*, signifies both delivering one's self to the community as an *arrepentido* and delivering one's self to God as a sinner in need of redemption.[85] The transformation sought is ambitious, and it reflects the fact that such religiously rooted rituals may dare to go into realms of social repair that secular paradigms do (but should not) fear entering.

Todd Whitmore, in an essay highlighting cultural forms of Christianity—such as among the Acholi of northern Uganda—that are capable of extending mercy even to perpetrators of political violence, invokes the phrase "magical Catholicism."[86] By this, he means not the typical dismissive reference to superstitious tribal religion, but rather a skill by which communities are able to follow and imitate Jesus' spiritual and social mission into the enemy territory of "the wicked." This mission can be scandalous, since, according to John Meier, "the damaging charge against [Jesus] was not that he associated with the poor but that he associated with the wicked."[87] Whitmore clarifies that in fact Jesus' "option for the poor" *and* his "option for the wicked" are both central to the gospel.[88] Nonetheless, in Peru, even among those who embrace the cause of the Andean poor, it would be tough to find support for pastoral outreach to the "wicked" perpetrators of political violence. Yet, ironically, this is precisely what many

84. Theidon, "Justice in Transition," 449.

85. Ibid., 451.

86. Whitmore, "Bridging Jesus' Missions," 202–3.

87. Ibid., 193–94.

88. Ibid., 196–97.

Andean poor communities have done, through the resources of their "magical Catholicism." I should note here that, in fact, many of the villages also display strong elements of Evangelical Christianity, yet, in the marshalling of spiritual and social resources to redeem the wicked, the skill set is the same. And one key skill in this set, directly related to the penitential ethic, should be adopted more robustly by civil society. If it is, while it may not produce the magical Andean result of "making new people," it will serve key goals of the Peruvian CVR.

The skill most on display in the villages, and most in need on the national stage, is the ability to inculcate a contrition that produces a desire for reconciliation. The Andean communities exercised this skill, as we saw, not by neglecting punishment but by placing it in the context of a hopeful, holistic, and reintegrative process. This process is best described as penance since the *arrepentidos* were engaged in practices through which they lamented, took responsibility for, and sought to repair the damage caused by their sins. But, more precisely, this inculcating skill was administered *as a gift*. This did not mean impunity. Noting "the logic of the gift," Theidon observes, "to receive a pardon is to be beholden" and "the *arrepentidos* would be reminded of this."[89] The community did not see reconciliation as something earned by perpetrators; rather, their view of reconciliation mirrored precisely Aquinas' formulation that it is a gift—to be practiced on God's terms. And that means that even the wicked, be they former *Senderistas* or former soldiers, receive a word of hope and the prospect of a new horizon, which can then propel new possibilities for participation in social repair.

89. Theidon, *Intimate Enemies*, 248.

7

Applying the Politics of Penance: Soldiers Returning from War

THE CRISIS OF U.S. troops returning from Iraq and Afghanistan is captured by news stories with just one term: PTSD. The sharp rise in diagnoses of post-traumatic stress disorder, and the military's efforts to take it more seriously, have come in response to an epidemic of suicides among military veterans. Most noteworthy of all statistics was the figure reported by the Veterans Administration itself in its 2012 Suicide Data Report. The report studied suicides over a four-year period and came to a shocking conclusion:

> Among cases where history of U.S. military service was reported, Veterans comprised approximately 22.2% of all suicides reported during the project period. If this prevalence estimate is assumed to be constant across all U.S. states, an estimated 22 Veterans will have died from suicide each day in the calendar year 2010.[1]

The report and the reactions to it within the military, government, and media have focused on the need to improve access to mental health care within the VA system. And yet, while treatment of PTSD is a necessary feature of the response to this crisis, more work is needed to identify the nature of the crisis. Indeed, an increasing number of veterans as well as clinical professionals are suggesting that, by itself, the PTSD diagnosis does not reach to the root of what often is a moral crisis—and what, in fact, may not even be a disorder but rather a properly human response to the evil of war. It is to this level of moral injury, and its repair, that I propose the penitential ethic.

---

1. Kemp and Bossarte, "Suicide Data Report, 2012," 15.

In his book *War and the Soul*, clinical psychotherapist Edward Tick recounts twenty-five years of work with veterans and emphasizes that "PTSD is not best understood or treated as a stress disorder" but rather "as an identity disorder and soul wound, affecting the personality at the deepest level."[2] In fact, PTSD is simply the latest iteration in a difficult attempt to name the constellation of pain associated with participation in war. Other historical terms in the American lexicon have been "soldier's heart," "shell shock," "battle fatigue," "the iron monkey," and "the thousand-yard stare."[3] To this list, Shawn Storer has added St. Augustine's term, *animi dolore*, the "anguish of the soul" that often comes in response to war. Storer notes that the real post-combat disorder may apply to those *not* experiencing *animi dolore*, which for Augustine *ought to* afflict those who experience "such great evils, such horror and cruelty."[4] The absence of such anguish is, according to Ausgutine, a fate "still more miserable" in that it could signal that one "has lost all human feeling."[5]

Attention to the wounds of soldiers is deeply rooted in Christian tradition, which developed postwar penitential strategies to heal and reintegrate soldiers returning from war. Such practices are in dire need today, and I will now sketch a trajectory of how my penitential ethic can promote social repair for the nation's veterans and the society to which they return. As with the previous cases, my hope is to stoke our political imagination, widen the scope of public reason on the topic, and motivate individuals to work for social repair of this pressing challenge. And, once again, I will deploy in specific ways the three main elements of my definition of penance—lament, responsibility, and reparation—to yield an ethic of overlapping practices and principles. The principle that comes to the fore in this case is social solidarity, which drives us as a community to support those who carry the moral burdens of a war fought in our name.

Lament: Learning to Listen

Dr. Warren Kinghorn, a psychiatrist in the Veterans Administration and a theologian at Duke University, warns against taking too lightly the task of listening to soldiers returning from war:

2. Tick, *War and the Soul*, 5.
3. Storer, "That Christ May Save Them," 2.
4. Ibid. See Augustine, *City of God*, XIX, 7.
5. Ibid.

> We need to find a way to help veterans narrate and experience their participation in combat as the properly human and morally laden activity that it is. This sounds easy, but it is not. Listening—really listening—to combat veterans is a hard thing to do. It is costly and many of the things our culture does ostensibly to support combat vets are, in the end, ways of not listening to them.[6]

While previous generations often did not know what to do with troubled veterans, American culture today adopts an increasingly standard response: the diagnosis and treatment of PTSD. And yet clinicians such as Kinghorn and Tick report that this is not enough and may even prevent the kinds of listening that returning soldiers need. Tick affirms the definition of PTSD first accepted by the American Psychiatric Association in 1980, which named "the critical factor of a catastrophic stressor out of the individual's control that threatened severe harm or death and would evoke similar responses in anyone" and that "results in biochemical imbalances and impaired neurological and cerebral functioning."[7] The problem is lack of attention to the roots of this neurological crisis, and, for this reason, many veterans "will not cooperate with medication regimens—often as a form of protest."[8] He reports his sessions with one soldier who described himself as "a walking chemistry experiment" and asked of his commanding officer, "Why doesn't he talk about my nightmares and memories and dead friends instead of asking how my meds are doing?"[9]

Tick hears a "common lament" from veterans: "Why can't I be who I was before?"[10] This lament is not nostalgia but rather involves "dimensions of the soul, the part of us that responds to morality, spirituality, aesthetics, and intimacy."[11] Unlike "almost all cultures and spiritual traditions of the world," our society does not have established processes to hear the soulful cries of soldiers.[12] Perhaps it is our desire to evade or rationalize the moral implications of the killing enterprise of war, but the soldier must face them: "The soul freezes on this moral crisis point. It says, I killed my own. Or, I killed whom I should not have killed and that is murder. I have become foul

---

6. Cited in Storer, "That Christ May Save Them," 3.

7. Tick, *War and the Soul*, 102.

8. Ibid.

9. Ibid.

10. Ibid., 106

11. Ibid., 108.

12. Ibid.

and cannot get clean again."[13] Tick does not believe that all wars are wrong or that all killing is wrong or even that all soldiers experience moral trauma, but experience gives him deep skepticism of societal attempts to name all returning troops unqualified heroes: "The soul knows the difference. PTSD tries to tell us."[14] While PTSD treatment can be construed as a way to avoid "dredging up" bad memories, storytelling is, in fact, a powerful tool of healing, especially when done "in a way that transfers the moral weight of the event from the individual [alone] to the community."[15]

Tick's insight strikes deep resonance with the penitential tradition, especially the principle—on display in Pope John Paul II's Jubilee laments—that remembering a painful past should be a communal enterprise. More particularly, his concept of "purification of memory," as the International Theological Commission noted, is a constructive task of "personal and collective conscience." The goal here is neither to suppress nor to alter history, but rather to heal the "resentment or violence left by the inheritance of the past."[16] Thus, what John Paul II meant by purification was placing painful memories into a social and eschatological horizon of hope. In the context of persons suffering most acutely from those memories, and thus with the least capacity for hope, the presence of a community to witness to the reality of this horizon is vital for healing to occur. These insights are particularly relevant in the case of soldiers. Not only are they uniquely burdened by the experiences of war, but they also are acting as agents of the community. Just as John Paul II was careful neither to posit nor to delete historical guilt in the case of actors associated with the sins lamented, so, too, the first step here must be a kind of solidarity by which we listen to laments that arise in our own context of two wars. This is not to say that soldiers lose their individual moral agency or personal responsibility for their actions—these too are key principles of the penitential ethic and will be addressed below—but rather that the first step is a shared one.

On a practical level, the task of listening can be promoted through a variety of means that display the need for recourse to practices from multiple traditions, especially religion and the arts. One initiative, led by Iraq War veteran and singer-songwriter Jason Moon, involves the use of art and music in a retreat setting. Over the course of four days, veterans share their

13. Ibid., 115.

14. Ibid., 118.

15. Ibid., 223.

16. International Theological Commission, *Memory and Reconciliation*, 5.1

stories, crafting them with Moon's help into songs and pieces of art, which are then displayed for the public on the last night of the retreat. "None of them, none, arrive ready for anyone—family, friend or stranger—to hear their story. It is often buried in shame and moral pain. But by the end, they claim the narrative and offer it to the community."[17] Attentive listening and creative enactment have not only brought veterans, including Moon himself, back from the brink of suicide but also have promoted further healing of wounds to the soul. Other efforts are more religiously rooted. In particular, Mennonite Church USA, the Archdiocese of Chicago, and the Catholic Peace Fellowship (CPF) all have initiatives of ministry to returning soldiers. Storer, the director of CPF, emphasizes that the goal of ministering to veterans cannot simply be to make them feel better. He is wary of a "therapeutic culture" that too quickly redirects feelings of guilt and shame. In contrast, "as the Church, we need to strive to listen to those returning from combat and take their moral pain and *animi dolore* seriously."[18] On a more secular plane, Paula Caplan of Harvard's Du Bois Institute has initiated a national listening project so that soldiers' stories can be shared, an initiative that is rooted in her 2011 book, *When Johnny and Jane Come Marching Home*. Whether in the church or in the arts or in secular settings, listening to veterans is a way of removing their isolation—and our isolation from the moral implications of war.

One final observation helps sharpen the need for the practice of lament I am proposing. The PTSD framework conditions us to focus on experiences that happen *to* the soldier—explosions, seeing comrades killed, being under fire. But Kinghorn argues that in addition to this "recipient trauma" there is also "agentic trauma" in which what troubles the soldier is not so much "what they witnessed, but what they *did*."[19] Even in situations in which soldiers were "under command" or under duress, psychologists report that moral agency is experienced and moral pain is felt, even if rarely verbalized.[20] The 2010 book *The Untold War* by Nancy Sherman indicates that the need for this kind of lament may be greater than we think. In a chapter titled "The Guilt They Carry"—which comes after she establishes the lengths to which the military goes to prepare soldiers to accept killing—she reports on her interviews with war veterans. Far more common

17 Personal interview, January 18, 2014.

18. Storer, "That Christ May Save Them," 13.

19. Cited in ibid., 9.

20. See ibid.

than the rationalizations society offers for the ugliness of war were phrases such as "If only I hadn't" and "If only I could have."[21] She even dismisses the "philosopher's term of art, 'agent-regret,'" which tries to capture a sense of moral remorse without culpability. Instead, she insists that what describes many soldiers' feelings is "the sheer weight of guilt—its heaviness, its identification with the victim, and the assertion of the need for repair."[22]

Responsibility: The Case for Postwar Penance

Few in the public discourse today would openly recommend for soldiers the traditional remedy for moral guilt: penance. Fewer still would retain one element of the traditional understanding of what that penance is: punishment. Of course, the problem with mentioning punishment in the context of returning soldiers is that they were operating with constrained moral agency within a command structure. And it can be hypocritical in the extreme to speak of the punishment of soldiers for the massive loss of life in wars fought on our behalf and with our money. Even if it seems odd that so many thousands can be killed and no one punished, simply because it occurred in war, a singular focus on soldiers risks making them a kind of scapegoat on whom we lay the moral guilt we all share. Nonetheless, the evidence suggests that, existentially, those soldiers are feeling that guilt more acutely and are enacting, most clearly in suicide, their own forms of punishment on themselves. In this sense, to ignore the question of moral responsibility does them a disservice. And, in fact, Christian tradition has long maintained the insight that soldiers, in a special way, ought to undergo a penitential discipline after returning from war. Even if it is better, and I think it is, not to refer such forms of discipline as "punishment"—unless we are willing to reclaim the concept entirely from dominant paradigms today—it is helpful to look at such historical practices and ask why they were seen as necessary.

In *The Moral Treatment of Returning Warriors*, Bernard Verkamp details the medieval imposition of penances after war. The tradition began as a retrieval of earlier practices, such as St. Basil's recommendation that returning soldiers "abstain from communion for three years."[23] Verkamp notes that while some objected to punishing soldiers, even ones who had

21. Sherman, *Untold War*, 92.

22. Ibid., 99.

23. Verkamp, *Moral Treatment of Returning Warriors*, 17.

fought justly, the penances came to be accepted and applied after all wars, "just as well as unjust."[24] Specific expectations were laid out in diverse ways through the many penitential texts of the early Middle Ages, with some imposing forty-day penances during Lent and others specifying various forms of fasting. The most detailed, and perhaps historically significant, set of prescriptions came in response to the Battle of Hastings in 1066. Among the penances imposed by a synod of Norman bishops, and approved by a papal legate, were the following:

- Anyone who knows that he killed a man in the great battle must do penance for one year for each man that he killed.

- Anyone who wounded a man, and does not know whether he killed him or not, must do penance for forty days for each man he thus struck.

- Those who fought merely for gain are to know that they owe penance as for a homicide.[25]

In this and other texts, what is envisioned by "penance" is most likely prayer, fasting, and alms. But alongside the call to *poenitere*, no mention is given of what the Irish monks had in earlier times called *satis facere*, acts of material and moral reparation for the damage done. Moreover, Verkamp notes that as the Middle Ages progressed, even less attention was given to penance for returning soldiers—no mention of it appears, for example, in Aquinas' *Summa*. Still, the practice does not disappear. As late as the sixteenth century, Charles Borromeo would include in his main penitential text a Lenten penance proper to returning warriors.[26]

Another resource for reflection on postwar penitential practices comes even more explicitly from the monastic tradition. As we saw with the Irish monks, monasteries were places that not only prescribed penances but also prescribed the location where some of them were carried out by penitents in residence for varied lengths of time. Historian Katherine Allen Smith, in her book *War and the Making of Medieval Monastic Culture*, reports that indeed monasteries were widely seen as spaces "where the bloodstained souls of worldly warriors could be washed clean through purifying spiritual

---

24. Ibid., 18

25. Ibid., 21–22.

26. Ibid., 23.

combat."[27] In part, this reflected monks' views of killing as shameful, a notion captured in the medieval monastic phrase "militia, id est, malitia," the military is malice.[28] Even after greater acceptance of the justifiability of war came into monastic consciousness, returning warriors were still drawn to monasteries. Smith notes that as wars proliferated, there were "ever larger numbers of penitent warriors who sought entrance" as monks.[29] This trend continued for centuries; the ranks of American monasteries, for instance, swelled after the Second World War. But, in medieval times, the connection was even clearer, as the soldier-turned-monk would be disarmed, signaling his "rebirth as a man of peace, in the image of Christ."[30] Smith, citing the work of Mayke de Jong, also notes that, in general, penitents could enter a "semi-monastic state," with a renunciation of arms and turn to peace included, though it is not clear that these penances were imposed specifically on returning soldiers.[31]

More study on this question is needed, but what is most important here is the rationale that contrasted the penitential disciplines of the monastery with the practices of war. Verkamp believes that the medievals were responding to the ancient "horror sanguinis," abhorrence of bloodshed.[32] On this point Smith concurs, noting that even among non-pacifists there was a strong conviction that soldiering "cannot be carried out without some doing of evil."[33] This consistent assessment from the penitential tradition tracks the empirical evidence compiled by Sherman. She uses the concept of collateral guilt to illustrate the experience by which some soldiers—individuals who broke no rule of war—take moral responsibility for war.[34] Sherman points out that in the "urban counterinsurgency" strategies of Iraq, soldiers were to establish "a sustainable civic order," a role that heightened their moral responsibility for civilians in their midst.[35] When "collateral damage" then occurred, the moral pain and guilt could be excruciating. Even in the absence of monastic penances, individuals like Sgt. Rob

---

27. Smith, *War and the Making of Medieval Monastic Culture*, 51.

28. Ibid.

29. Ibid.

30. Ibid., 62.

31. Ibid., 63.

32. Verkamp, *Moral Treatment of Returning Warriors*, 24.

33. Smith, *War and the Making of Medieval Monastic Culture*, 50.

34. Sherman, *Untold War*, 107–10.

35. Ibid., 108.

Sarra were compelled to renounce their arms as a way of coping with their moral responsibility for killing. In 2003, Sarra fired on an Iraqi woman who, he feared, might be a suicide bomber at a checkpoint. "When she hit the ground, there was a white flag in her hand. . . . And I was like, 'Oh, my God.'"[36] She was unable, it seems, to understand the Marines' attempts to shout "stop" in Arabic. Though exonerated by his command—which even concluded that it was likely not his shot that killed her—and though given counseling and rest, Sarra was so stricken by guilt that he was sent back to the States and given a discharge, ending his military career.

I am not suggesting that Rob Sarra should be punished for his role in this killing. Yet, his own moral inventory suggests that he should be asked to assume some measure of responsibility. Even Sherman—who, as an ethicist for the military, is no pacifist—sees the need for soldiers like him to "reclaim a sense of personal agency and moral autonomy minimized by putting on a uniform."[37] Responding to and reinforcing this individual moral agency—so evident in the penitential approach of the Irish monks— is for Sherman a way in which returning warriors can "reaffirm their own humanity."[38] She does not offer a particular strategy by which this can happen, but I have argued that the practice of penance can be applied to this need. My case, rooted in the penitential tradition, has been that when measures to preserve the individual moral agency of soldiers are enmeshed in practices of social solidarity by which the rest of us share that responsibility, the result is a deeply layered approach to social repair.

The rationale here is not punitive—though, for some actors, such as political leaders, it is not improper to speak of punishment—and the program I suggest falls more squarely within the practice of reparation in the penitential ethic, especially since it will involve the people of Iraq and Afghanistan. It is that concluding proposal that I now offer.

Reparation for War and "The War after the War"

Increasingly, ethicists and political scientists are asking questions about *ius post bellum*, justice after war. This development is promising, raising awareness about the responsibility to create stable structures of peace and suggesting new ways to hold political leaders and states accountable for the

36. Ibid., 109.
37. Ibid., 110.
38. Ibid.

human and ecological damage of war.[39] Work in this area is broad-ranging and could include questions as diverse as "What is the obligation of the Iraqi or Afghan states to compensate victims of the brutal regimes ousted by war?" and "Does the United States owe reparations for the devastation it has visited on these countries?" These are important topics of transitional justice and international law, but I wish here to propose practices that, while not enforceable by legal mechanisms, could also promote deep forms of reconciliation that respond both to the wounds of Iraqi and Afghan citizens who have suffered the wars and to the wounds of U.S. soldiers who have prosecuted it.

Given the insistence in the penitential ethic that social solidarity support individual moral agency, I begin at the communal level with the suggestion of a statement of collective lament directed to the peoples of Iraq and Afghanistan. Ideally, this would build on the domestic work of listening to the laments of soldiers returning from war. And this does not necessarily mean apology—recall that John Paul II's expressions were not precisely apologies—but it does include expressions of heartfelt grief and an acknowledgment of moral agency, that the sufferings caused were not mere "accidents." This form of repentance could be initiated at any level, from groups of soldiers to the president, as a way to carry together the moral burden of war and to commit to the repair of its damage. I do not pretend that the political will for this initiative is presently evident—and likely some soldiers without moral injury would be initially offended—and so the case must be made. For the many soldiers isolated in the kind of guilt described by Sherman, the expression of communal repentance could be a powerful move toward the restoration of right relationship, with fellow Americans as well as those in the land where they fought. Moreover, as the powerful witness of John Paul displayed, even unpopular acts of repentance—which his was in many internal circles—can unleash a cascade of subsidiary movements toward moral and social repair.

Such a message would not require a political resolution of the intractable questions surrounding the justice of the respective wars. Rather, the collective lament would be directed at the losses and wounds of all affected by the war. There is also some political precedence for this kind of action. President Bill Clinton's famous 1998 speech in Rwanda was marked by a general penitence for "the capacity for people everywhere" to do and

---

39. See Allman and Winright, *After the Smoke Clears.*

tolerate evil.[40] He noted the moral culpability of Rwandans but also admitted that "we"—and here his reference was not even to the U.S. alone but to "the international community"—"must bear [our] share of responsibility." Though no apology was explicitly made, Clinton's words gave validity to the need for repentance on many levels in the wake of the crisis. In the context of the wars in Iraq and Afghanistan, a collective lament could be powerfully productive of moral and material repair, even if the statement stopped short of apology. My point is not even so much that the initiative must come from the president—an unlikely scenario indeed—but that the greater the communal participation and solidarity in the practice, the more effective it will be. This was the real genius of John Paul's many gestures of collective penitence—so many of them delivered at the sites of former enmity and war—since only in retrospect could we see the freedom it gave individuals to take part in undoing the pain of the past.

Thus, the second suggestion focuses on opportunities for soldiers themselves to participate in reparation. Here recent precedence is more evident, though the current paradigm needs to be challenged. In 2009, the *New York Times* first reported on Operation Proper Exit, a program privately funded but with the approval of the USO and General Ray Odierno, then the highest-ranking commander in Iraq.[41] Previously kept under wraps due to security concerns but now promoted publicly, Operation Proper Exit is a seven-day experience for veterans who either left Iraq rapidly, by medical evacuation, or traumatically, by the loss of comrades' lives. The hope is that "returning to places many of them left while unconscious or in agony might reassure them that their losses have been worth it."[42] And many do experience relief, especially if they see improvements in the security or social situation where they had served. Colonel David Sutherland reported of fellow trip members that "some of them said their night terrors stopped after they went" and that he himself "left about 15 pounds of guilt back in Iraq after that trip."[43]

The idea and especially the name of Operation Proper Exit are promising and point to possibilities for similar initiatives—which do exist but

40. President Bill Clinton, "Remarks to the People of Rwanda," March 25, 1998. For the text of Clinton's speech, see http://www.cbsnews.com/news/text-of-clintons-rwanda-speech/.

41. Nordland, "Wounded Soldiers Return to Iraq."

42. Ibid.

43. Ibid.

have not had nearly the same the resources or official support—which also include practices of restorative justice. Ex-Army Sergeant and Iraq War veteran Logan Mehl-Laituri returned to Iraq in 2010 as part of a peacemaking delegation. Though not without challenges, and ones particular to his experiences as a former soldier in that war, he affirms the restoring rationale of the trip.[44] Some of the soldiers, including Moon, who were featured in the 2011 documentary by Olivier Morel, *On the Bridge*, which presents the postwar struggle in their own words, traveled to Baghdad in 2013 to share the film with Iraqis. Another initiative, aimed at material restitution, is the Veterans for Peace Iraq Water Project, a response to damage on water supplies and treatment facilities inflicted by years of war and sanctions. The presently dangerous situation in Iraq has prevented more personal involvement of veterans in such projects, a fact that highlights the need for programs of repair that tend to Iraqis' wounds in ways that do not require the expensive and delicate coordination of trips. One such way would be to connect veterans to the large and growing community of Iraqi refugees in the United States. Establishing reciprocity and friendship in this venue can generate for soldiers a horizon of hope that the experience of targeting and killing Iraqis need not have the last word in their relationship. Such a project would embody precisely the concept of satisfaction put forward by Thomas Aquinas.

It would also employ a key insight of John Paul II and the ITC, which emphasized the necessity that gestures of repentance move to "gestures of reparation."[45] In a general sense, this insight is widely recognized by veterans. A group known as The Mission Continues was founded in 2007 by soldiers who had returned from Iraq seeking a way to motivate those who had been wounded physically and psychologically. The group places veterans in service projects from neighborhood cleanups to disaster relief.[46] The basic principle at work is that the process of reintegration into society should not, for soldiers, have to mean leaving behind the mission orientation and martial virtues that have been cultivated for so long. Rather, these skills can be redeployed in a reparative way. Within a penitential ethic of social repair as well as the framework of restorative justice, the benefits of these programs would be even stronger if they were tied more directly to the good of members of the society in which the former soldiers were at

44. See Barrett, *The Gospel of Rutba*.

45. Ibid.

46. Klein, "Can Service Save Us?," 24–34.

war. In this way, and especially for soldiers experiencing moral injury, the reparation would address not only the wounds of war but also those of what one soldier described to Sherman as "the war after war."[47]

I will now offer a final suggestion, which addresses not the repair of soldiers but the way in which their experiences call us to repair ourselves—and specifically, our political reliance on recourse to war. In *Packing Inferno: The Unmaking of a Marine*, Iraq War veteran Tyler Boudreau recounts his combat experience and the moral hell that he internalized after he returned home. In the book's conclusion, he reflects on the well-known challenge faced by everyone from the VA to churches to get veterans to seek help for war trauma, to "show up" for support group meetings or information sessions. For a long while, he says, it struck him as curious that, while the system is flooded with cries for help from the brink of suicide or breakdown, few soldiers (including himself) seem interested in the many well-intentioned offers of "decent folks, churchgoers, community members" who ask "with genuine sympathy: how can we help?"[48] Ultimately, he realized that the problem is assumptions about who is most in need of repair. And so to the question, "How can we help?" he concluded,

> I say they can't help. They can't help as long as they carry the nagging assumption that it is the veteran's consciousness that has become deranged—not their own. . . . They will get as touchy-feely as a man could ever stomach, but they won't get tough. They won't point their fingers at the most obvious issue and say, "War did this. Now why do we have war?" For most people the answer is too costly to find. There is simply too much to lose. . . . And that is why they can never truly and completely address the veteran's illness. As long as combat stress remains in the category of "tragic necessity," we will never be able to cure it.[49]

What Boudreau is pointing to is a kind of "war privilege," analogous to the concept of "white privilege" discussed by Pfeil in connection to hyperincarceration. The benefits we perceive, consciously or not, from having a massive fighting force act in our name establish norms against raising moral questions with soldiers—questions that we think *they* might not want to answer but that in truth *we* do not want to answer. It is not, Boudreau notes, that veterans are looking for antiwar PTSD counseling, but rather that an

47. Sherman, *Untold War*, 210.
48. Boudreau, *Packing Inferno*, 211.
49. Ibid., 213.

implicit acceptance of war places myriad "barriers" to stories that need to be told. The soldier, he says, "has expectations to live up to—his own, the military's, his family's, his friends', and everyone else" who draws a line at questioning the morality of war itself.[50]

Boudreau's challenge is to create a framework in which the voices of returning soldiers can help repair us, addressing our destructive reliance on war. As a practical strategy, this reverses the roles of "soldier as patient, sensitive civilian as healer" and empowers veterans as moral agents with an important witness to share with society—indeed, it is our only real way "to know what war actually is."[51] He is aware that the results will be ambiguous, since soldiers do not return with a uniform narrative of the meaning of war. But "that's good" because their stories (including the ugly ones) "capture the struggle" to address "the ethical problem of war."[52] In this way, soldiers and their stories can become "the healing stones of society" in addressing the root cause of moral injury in the first place: war.[53]

This way of seeing the task of reintegrating soldiers brings a new and final dimension to the value of penance and the penitential ethic. Through the work of listening to soldiers, all of us can lament, take responsibility for, and seek to repair the wounds of war, which not only afflict the souls of soldiers but also the body politic. If the task of reintegration included this kind of listening—on a level both wide and deep—it would embody all three principles of the penitential ethic. Interpersonal engagement with returning soldiers would generate fresh motivations for the repair of wounds and would promote broad communal engagement in repentance after war—and without the kind of condescension that pathologizes soldiers and transfers moral burdens to them. Indeed, in this paradigm, it is soldiers—with their suffering, even their sins—who can help to heal us from the moral injury that war inflicts on us as a people.

Through each of my case studies, I have proposed and applied the penitential ethic for social repair. The three distinct but interrelated contexts illustrate the need for the three distinct but interrelated elements of my construal of penance as practices through which persons lament, take responsibility for, and seek to repair the wounds caused by sin. The epidemic of suicide among veterans returning from war shows, in a special way,

50. Ibid., 216.
51. Ibid.
52. Ibid., 117–18
53. Ibid.

the need to more effectively listen to displays of *lament*, in particular those of soldiers with deep moral injury. The principle—gleaned from the power of Pope John Paul II's Jubilee laments—that supports this practice is communal solidarity. The failures and injustices of the American prison system highlight the need to better help persons *take responsibility for* criminal action, a task that involves refining the concept of punishment that drives our system. The principle—drawn from the Irish monks and their promotion of medicinal punishment—that frames this strategy is the preservation of individual moral agency for all those affected by crime: offenders, victims, and the whole of society. Finally, macro-level failures of transitional justice in Peru, especially affecting marginalized victim-survivors in the Andes, reveal the need to better generate commitments to *seek to repair the wounds* that were left by the conflict. The principle—drawn from the theology of Thomas Aquinas—that most clearly propels this strategy centers on the importance of a horizon of new hope in the daunting task of reparation.

I intend the penitential ethic not simply as a series of suggestions or projects through which to tackle each of the cases. I have included some specific recommendations in order to show that the ethic is ordered toward practice and not mere theory. Still, I am aware that many of my suggestions—such as a collective lament for the peoples of Iraq and Afghanistan—will be dismissed as politically improbable. Others—such as the consideration of forms of amnesty in Peru—will rightly be challenged within competing visions of transitional justice. And a few—such as expansion of restorative justice programs in the wake of crime—will not be new at all but rather part of significant programs already begun. Thus, it is important to clarify that, more than simply producing action items in a plan, the penitential ethic is designed to inform the way we think about social repair. In this way, as I explained in the theology of political engagement I presented in the first chapter, my goal has been to stoke our imagination by presenting resources that are both rooted in religious tradition and relevant for the civic arena. If I have succeeded in that task, then persons with a vast array of roles in society will be able to see more clearly the repairing power available in the politics of penance.

Bibliography

Accattoli, Luigi. *When a Pope Asks Forgiveness: The Mea Culpa's of John Paul II.* Translated by Jordan Aumann. New York: Alba House, 1998.

Accattoli, Luigi, et al. *John Paul II: A Pope for the People.* Translated by Russell Stockman. New York: Harry N. Abrams, 2004.

Alexander, Michelle. *The New Jim Crow: Mass Incarceration in the Age of Colorblindness.* New York: Perseus, 2012.

Allen, John L., Jr. *The Future Church: How Ten Trends Are Revolutionizing the Catholic Church.* New York: Doubleday, 2009.

Allman, Mark J., and Tobias L. Winright. *After the Smoke Clears: The Just War Tradition and Post War Justice.* Maryknoll, NY: Orbis, 2010.

America. "Asking Forgiveness." March 25, 2000. http://americamagazine.org/issue/281/editorial/asking-forgiveness.

Anderson, Gary A. *Sin: A History.* New Haven: Yale University Press, 2009.

Aquinas, Thomas. *Scriptum super libros Sententiarum magistri Petri Lombardi.* Paris: Lethielleux, 1929.

————. *Summa theologiae.* Translated by Fathers of the English Dominican Province. 1955. http://www.newadvent.org/summa/.

Aristotle. *Nichomachean Ethics.* Translated by Martin Ostwald. Indianapolis: Bobbs-Merrill, 1962.

Barrett, Greg. *The Gospel of Rutba: War, Peace, and the Good Samaritan Story in Iraq.* Maryknoll, NY: Orbis, 2012.

Benedict XV, Pope. *Pacem, Dei Munus Pulcherrimum.* May 23, 1920. http://w2.vatican.va/content/benedict-xv/en/encyclicals/documents/hf_ben-xv_enc_23051920_pacem-dei-munus-pulcherrimum.html.

Benedict XVI, Pope. *God Is Love—Deus Caritas Est: Encyclical Letter.* Vatican City: Libreria Editrice Vaticana, 2006.

Bergen, Jeremy M. *Ecclesial Repentance: The Churches Confront Their Sinful Pasts.* London: T. & T. Clark, 2011.

Bernardin, Joseph. "New Rite of Penance Suggested." *Origins* 13 (1983) 324–26.

Bieler, Ludwig. "The Irish Penitentials: Their Religious and Social Background." *Studia Patristica* 8 (1966) 329–33.

BIBLIOGRAPHY

Biemer, John. "US Catholic Hierarchy Asks Forgiveness for Past Sins." Associated Press, December 29, 2000. https://news.google.com/newspapers?nid=348&dat=20001229&id=szEwAAAAIBAJ&sjid=uDsDAAAAIBAJ&pg=3829,4406649&hl=en.

Bonhoeffer, Dietrich. *The Cost of Discipleship*. New York: Simon and Schuster, 1995.

————. *Life Together; Prayerbook of the Bible*. Edited by Geffrey B. Kelly. Translated by Daniel W. Bloesch and James H. Burtness. Dietrich Bonhoeffer Works 5. Minneapolis: Fortress, 1996.

Boudreau, Tyler E. *Packing Inferno: The Unmaking of a Marine*. Port Townsend, WA: Feral House, 2008.

Braithwaite, John. "Restorative Justice: Theories and Worries." Visiting Experts' Papers, 123rd International Senior Seminar, Resource Material Series No. 63. Tokyo: United Nations Asia and Far East Institute for the Prevention of Crime and the Treatment of Offenders, 2004. http://www.unafei.or.jp/english/pdf/PDF_rms/no63/ch05.pdf.

Braman, Donald. *Doing Time on the Outside: Incarceration and Family Life in Urban America*. Ann Arbor: University of Michigan Press, 2007.

Brett, Annabel S. *Liberty, Right and Nature: Individual Rights in Later Scholastic Thought*. Cambridge: Cambridge University Press, 2003.

Brooks, Peter. *Troubling Confessions: Speaking Guilt in Law and Literature*. Chicago: University of Chicago Press, 2000.

Burt, Jo-Marie. "Análisis de las sentencias emitidas por el Poder Judicial en Juicios por Derechos Humanos en el Perú." http://rightsperu.net/index.php/human-rights-trials-in-peru-juicios-por-derechos-humanos/resumenes-de-casos/153-casos-de-violaciones-de-derechos-humanos-en-en-el-peru-resumenes-case-summaries-of-human-rights-trials-in-peru.

————. "Fujimori's Trial: A Process That Has Been Exemplary." *CEJIL.org.*, November 24, 2009. https://cejil.org/en/comunicados/fujimoris-trial-a-process-has-been-exemplary.

Bushlack, Thomas J. "Justice in the Theology of Thomas Aquinas: Rediscovering Civic Virtue." PhD diss., University of Notre Dame, 2011.

Cahill, Thomas. *How the Irish Saved Civilization: The Untold Story of Ireland's Heroic Role from the Fall of Rome to the Rise of Medieval Europe*. New York: Doubleday, 1995.

Caplan, Paula J. *When Johnny and Jane Come Marching Home: How All of Us Can Help Veterans*. Cambridge: MIT Press, 2011.

Casas, Bartolomé de las. *Confesionario*. In *Indian Freedom: The Cause of Bartolomé de Las Casas, 1484–1566: A Reader*, translated by Francis Patrick Sullivan, 282–88. Kansas City: Sheed & Ward, 1995.

————. *De unico vocationis modo*. Madrid: Alianza, 1990.

Catholic Church. *Catechism of the Catholic Church*. Washington, DC: United States Catholic Conference, 1994.

Cessario, Romanus. *Christian Satisfaction in Aquinas: Towards a Personalist Understanding*. Washington, DC: University Press of America, 1982.

Charles-Edwards, T. M. "The Penitential of Columbanus." In *Columbanus: Studies on the Latin Writings*, edited by Michael Lapidge, 217–39. Woodbridge, UK: Boydell, 1997.

Comisión de la Verdad y Reconciliación. *Conclusiones y recomendaciones: Informe final de la Comisión de la Verdad y Reconciliación*. Lima, Perú. http://www.cverdad.org.pe/ingles/ifinal/conclusiones.php.

Committee on the Judiciary, U.S. House of Representatives. "Defining the Problem and Scope of Over-criminalization and Over-federalization." Serial No. 113–44. Washington, DC: U.S. Government Printing Office, 2013.

Connolly, Hugh. *Irish Penitentials and Their Significance for the Sacrament of Penance Today*. Dublin: Four Courts, 1995.

Copeland, M. Shawn. "Political Theology as Interruptive." *CTSA Proceedings* 59 (2004) 71–82.

Correa, Cristián. "Making Concrete a Message of Inclusion: Reparations for Victims of Massive Crimes." In *Victimological Approaches to International Crimes: Africa*, edited by Rianne Letschert et al., 185–233. Portland: Intersentia, 2011.

———. "Reparations in Peru: From Recommendations to Implementation." International Center for Transitional Justice, June 2013. http://ictj.org/sites/default/files/ICTJ_Report_Peru_Reparations_2013.pdf.

Dallen, James. *The Reconciling Community: The Rite of Penance*. New York: Pueblo, 1986.

David, Roman, and Susanne Y. P. Choi. "Getting Even or Getting Equal? Retributive Desires and Transitional Justice." *Political Psychology* 30 (2009) 161–92.

De Greiff, Pablo, ed. *The Handbook of Reparations*. Oxford: Oxford University Press, 2006.

De Gruchy, John W. *Reconciliation: Restoring Justice*. Minneapolis: Fortress, 2002.

Dolcich-Ashley, Anselma T. "Precept, Rights and Ecclesial Governance: A Moral-Theological Analysis of the Catholic Sexual Abuse Crisis in the U.S." PhD diss., University of Notre Dame, 2011.

Dooley, Kate. "Women Confessors in the Middle Ages." *Louvain Studies* 20 (1995) 271–81.

Drake, Bruce. "Incarceration Gap Widens between Whites and Blacks." Pew Research Center. September 6, 2013. http://www.pewresearch.org/fact-tank/2013/09/06/incarceration-gap-between-whites-and-blacks-widens/.

Dulles, Avery. "Should the Church Repent?" *First Things*, December 1998. http://www.firstthings.com/article/1998/12/should-the-church-repent.

Du Plessis, Max. "Reparations and International Law: How Are Reparations to Be Determined (Past Wrong or Current Effects), against Whom, and What Form Should They Take?" *Windsor Yearbook of Access to Justice* 22 (2003) 41–69.

Du Plessis, Max, and Stephen Peté, eds. *Repairing the Past? International Perspectives on Reparations for Gross Human Rights Abuses*. Antwerpen: Intersentia, 2007.

Favazza, Joseph A. *The Order of Penitents: Historical Roots and Pastoral Future*. Collegeville, MN: Liturgical, 1988.

Filteau, Jerry. "Bishops to Fast, Pray, Aug. 14–15, Invite Catholics to Join In." *Catholic News Service*, June 26, 2002. http://www.freerepublic.com/focus/f-religion/798515/replies?c=1.

Forero, Juan. "Peru Truth Commission Stirs Up a Hornet's Nest." *International Herald Tribune*, September 9, 2003, 5.

Forest, Jim. *Confession: Doorway to Forgiveness*. Maryknoll, NY: Orbis, 2002.

Getek, Kathryn. "Just Punishment? A Virtue Ethics Approach to Prison Reform in the United States." PhD disss., Boston College, 2010.

Glazek, Christopher. "Raise the Crime Rate." *n +1*, January 26, 2012. http://nplusonemag.com/raise-the-crime-rate.

Glendon, Mary Ann. "Contrition in the Age of Spin Control." *First Things*, November 1997. http://www.firstthings.com/article/1997/11/002-contrition-in-the-age-of-spin-control.

Griffin, Michael. "Snubbed: Pope Benedict XV and Cardinal James Gibbons." *The Sign of Peace: Journal of the Catholic Peace Fellowship* 6.1 (2007). http://www.catholicpeacefellowship.org/downloads/BenedictXV_Gibbons.pdf.

Grossman, Cathy Lynn. "Clergy Sex Abuse Scandals Top $2.5 Billion Nationwide." *USA Today*, March 13, 2013. http://www.usatoday.com/story/news/nation/2013/03/13/sex-abuse-settlement-cardinal-roger-mahony/1984217/.

Gutiérrez, Gustavo. *Las Casas: In Search of the Poor of Jesus Christ.* Translated by Robert R. Barr. Maryknoll, NY: Orbis, 1993.

Hauerwas, Stanley. *With the Grain of the Universe.* Grand Rapids: Baker Academic, 2013.

Himes, Kenneth R., et al., eds. *Modern Catholic Social Teaching: Commentaries and Interpretations.* Washington, DC: Georgetown University Press, 2005.

Immarigeon, Russ. "Survey Reveals Broad Support for Alternative Sentencing." *National Prison Project Journal* 9 (1986) 1–4.

International Center for Transitional Justice. "Ten Years after Peru's Truth Commission." http://www.ictj.org/news/ten-years-after-peru-truth-commission.

International Theological Commission. *Memory and Reconciliation: The Church and the Faults of the Past.* December 1999. http://www.vatican.va/roman_curia/congregations/cfaith/cti_documents/rc_con_cfaith_doc_20000307_memory-reconc-itc_en.html.

Jaspers, Karl. *The Question of German Guilt.* Translated by E. B. Ashton. New York: Capricorn, 1961.

John Paul II, Pope. "Address of John Paul II to the Cardinals of the United States." April 23, 2002. http://w2.vatican.va/content/john-paul-ii/en/speeches/2002/april/documents/hf_jp-ii_spe_20020423_usa-cardinals.html.

———. *Christefidelis laici.* December 30, 1988. http://w2.vatican.va/content/john-paul-ii/en/apost_exhortations/documents/hf_jp-ii_exh_30121988_christifideles-laici.html.

———. "First Sunday of Lent 'Day of Pardon' Presentation." March 12, 2000. http://www.vatican.va/news_services/liturgy/documents/ns_lit_doc_20000312_presentation-day-pardon_en.html.

———. *Memory and Identity: Conversations at the Dawn of a Millennium.* New York: Rizzoli, 2005.

———. "Offer Forgiveness and Receive Peace: World Day of Peace Message." *Origins* 26 (1997) 453–58.

———. *On the Coming of the Third Millennium—Tertio Millennio Adveniente: Apostolic Letter, November 10, 1994.* Washington, DC: United States Catholic Conference, 1994.

———. "The Value of This Collegial Body." In *Penance and Reconciliation in the Mission of the Church.* Washington, DC: U.S. Catholic Conference, 1984.

Kant, Immanuel. *The Metaphysics of Morals.* Translated by Mary Gregor. Cambridge: Cambridge University Press, 1991.

Katongole, Emmanuel. "Born of Lament: On the Possibility and Prospects of Hope in Africa." Presentation at the University of Notre Dame, Notre Dame, Indiana, March 22, 2012.

Katongole, Emmanuel, and Chris Rice. *Reconciling All Things: A Christian Vision for Justice, Peace and Healing.* Downers Grove, IL: InterVarsity, 2008.

Keenan, James, and Thomas A. Shannon. *The Context of Casuistry.* Washington, DC: Georgetown University Press, 1995.

Kemp, Janet, and Robert Bossarte. "Suicide Data Report, 2012." Department of Veterans Affairs, Mental Health Services, Suicide Prevention Program. http://www.va.gov/opa/docs/Suicide-Data-Report-2012-final.pdf.

Kleiman, Mark A. R. *When Brute Force Fails: How to Have Less Crime and Less Punishment.* Princeton: Princeton University Press, 2010.

Klein, Joe. "Can Service Save Us?" *Time* 182.1 (2013) 24–34.

Lantigua, David M. "Idolatry, War, and the Rights of Infidels: The Christian Legal Theory of Religious Toleration in the New World." PhD diss., University of Notre Dame 2012.

Laplante, Lisa J., and Kimberly Theidon. "Truth with Consequences: Justice and Reparations in Post-Truth Commission Peru." *Human Rights Quarterly* 29 (2007) 228–50.

Liguori, Alfonso Maria de'. *Selected Writings.* Edited by Frederick M. Jones et al. New York: Paulist, 1999.

———. *Theologia Moralis.* Edited by L. Gaudé. 4 vols. Rome: Typographia Vaticana, 1905.

Lodonu, Francis. "Reconciliation and African Realities." *Origins* 13 (1983) 349–50.

Luijten, Eric. *Sacramental Forgiveness as a Gift of God: Thomas Aquinas on the Sacrament of Penance.* Leuven: Peeters, 2003.

Mahoney, John. *The Making of Moral Theology: A Study of the Roman Catholic Tradition.* Oxford: Oxford University Press, 1990.

Massingale, Bryan N. *Racial Justice and the Catholic Church.* Maryknoll, NY: Orbis, 2010.

Mattison, William C. *Introducing Moral Theology: True Happiness and the Virtues.* Grand Rapids: Brazos, 2008.

McNeill, John T., and Helena M. Gamer. *Medieval Handbooks of Penance: A Translation of the Principal "Libri Poenitentiales" and Selections from Related Documents.* New York: Columbia University Press, 1990.

Meehan, Bernard. *The Book of Kells: An Illustrated Introduction to the Manuscript in Trinity College, Dublin.* New York: Thames and Hudson, 1994.

Mikulich, Alexander, et al. *The Scandal of White Complicity in Us Hyper-incarceration: A Nonviolent Spirituality of White Resistance.* New York: Palgrave Macmillan, 2013.

Mills, Nicolaus. "The Modern Notion of a Public Apology." *Los Angeles Times,* March 19, 2000. http://articles.latimes.com/2000/mar/19/opinion/op-10413.

Mitchell, Gerard. "The Origins of Irish Penance." *Irish Theological Quarterly* 22 (1955) 1–14.

Mitchell, Nathan, ed. *The Rite of Penance: Commentaries.* Vol. 3, *Background and Directions.* Washington, DC: Liturgical, 1978.

Morrow, Maria. "Reconnecting Sacrament and Virtue: Penance in Thomas's *Summa Theologiae.*" *New Blackfriars* 91 (2010) 304–20.

Murphy, Jeffrie G., and Jean Hampton. *Forgiveness and Mercy.* Cambridge: Cambridge University Press, 1988.

Nordland, Rod. "Wounded Soldiers Return to Iraq, Seeking Solace." *New York Times,* October 15, 2009. http://www.nytimes.com/2009/10/15/world/middleeast/15exit.html?_r=0.

Onis, Paco de, et al. *State of Fear: The Truth about Terrorism.* New Day Films (DVD), 2005.

Orsy, Ladislas M. *The Evolving Church and the Sacrament of Penance.* Denville, NJ: Dimension Books, 1978.

Peru Support Group. *The Findings of Peru's Truth and Reconciliation Commission: A Summary.* London: PSG, 2004.

Pew Charitable Trusts. "Project Update: U.S. Prison Population Drops for Third Year as States Adopt New Policy Strategies." Pew Center on the States, August 8, 2013. http://www.pewtrusts.org/en/about/news-room/press-releases/2013/08/08/us-prison-population-drops-for-third-year-as-states-adopt-new-policy-strategies.

———. "Public Safety, Public Spending: Forecasting America's Prison Population 2007–2011." June 2007. http://www.jfa-associates.com/publications/ppsm/pspp_prison_projections_0207.pdf.

Pfeil, Margaret R. "Social Sin: Social Reconciliation?" In *Reconciliation, Nations and Churches in Latin America*, edited by Iain MacLean, 171–92. Burlington, VT: Ashgate, 2006.

———. "Toward an Understanding of the Language of Social Sin in Magisterial Teaching." PhD diss., University of Notre Dame, 2000.

Pfeil, Margaret R., and Tobias L Winright. *Violence, Transformation, and the Sacred: "They Shall Be Called Children of God"*. Maryknoll, NY: Orbis, 2012.

Philpott, Daniel. *Just and Unjust Peace: An Ethic of Political Reconciliation*. New York: Oxford University Press, 2012.

Pieper, Josef. *The Four Cardinal Virtues*. Translated by Richard Winston et al. 1st ed. Notre Dame: University of Notre Dame Press, 1966.

Pigou, Piers. "The Community Reconciliation Process of the Commission for Truth, Reception and Reconciliation." United Nations Development Program. http://www.cavr-timorleste.org/en/reconciliation.htm.

Pope, Stephen. "Accountability and Sexual Abuse in the United States: Lessons for the Universal Church." *Irish Theological Quarterly* 69 (2004) 73–88.

Porter, Jean. *Ministers of the Law: A Natural Law Theory of Legal Authority*. Grand Rapids: Eerdmans, 2010.

———. "The Virtue of Justice." In *The Ethics of Aquinas*, edited by Stephen J. Pope, 272–86. Washington, DC: Georgetown University Press, 2002.

Poschmann, Bernhard. *Penance and the Anointing of the Sick*. New York: Herder and Herder, 1964.

Pouligny, Béatrice, et al., eds. *After Mass Crime: Rebuilding States and Communities*. New York: United Nations University Press, 2007.

Ratzinger, Joseph. "The Necessity of Personal Confession." *Origins* 13 (1983) 331–32.

Rey-Mermet, Théodule. *Moral Choices: The Moral Theology of Saint Alphonsus Liguori*. Translated by Paul Laverdure. Liguori, MO: Liguori, 1998.

Riga, Peter J. *Sin and Penance: Insights into the Mystery of Salvation*. Milwaukee: Bruce, 1962.

Robinson, Walter V., et al. "Scores of Priests Involved in Sex Abuse Cases: Settlements Kept Scope of Issue out of Public Eye." *Boston Globe*, January 31, 2002. https://www.bostonglobe.com/news/special-reports/2002/01/31/scores-priests-involved-sex-abuse-cases/kmRm7JtqBdEZ8UF0ucR16L/story.html.

Schimmel, Solomon. *Wounds Not Healed by Time: The Power of Repentance and Forgiveness*. Oxford: Oxford University Press, 2002.

Schmemann, Alexander. "Some Reflections on Confession." *St. Vladimir's Seminary Quarterly* 5 (1961) 38–44.

Schreiter, Robert J. *The Ministry of Reconciliation: Spirituality & Strategies*. Maryknoll, NY: Orbis, 1998.

Schreiter, Robert J., et al., eds. *Peacebuilding: Catholic Theology, Ethics, and Praxis*. Maryknoll, NY: Orbis, 2010.

Schuck, Michael. "Early Modern Roman Catholic Social Thought, 1740–1890." In *Modern Catholic Social Teaching: Commentaries and Interpretations*, edited by Kenneth R. Himes et al., 99–124. Washington, DC: Georgetown University Press, 2005.

Searle, Mark. "The Journey of Conversion." *Worship* 54 (1980) 35–55.

Sherman, Nancy. *The Untold War: Inside the Hearts, Minds, and Souls of Our Soldiers*. New York: Norton, 2010.

Shubin, Daniel H. *Monastery Prisons*. Bloomington: Xlibris, 2001.

Skotnicki, Andrew. "Foundations Once Destroyed: The Catholic Church and Criminal Justice." *Theological Studies* 65 (2004) 792–816.

Smith, Katherine Allen. *War and the Making of Medieval Monastic Culture*. Suffolk, UK: Boydell, 2011.

Storer, Shawn. "That Christ May Save Them and Raise Them Up: Ministering to Those Returned from Combat with Animi Dolore." MDiv thesis, University of Notre Dame, 2012.

Theidon, Kimberly. *Intimate Enemies: Violence and Reconciliation in Peru*. Philadelphia: University of Pennsylvania Press, 2013.

———. "Justice in Transition: The Micropolitics of Reconciliation in Postwar Peru." *The Journal of Conflict Resolution* 50 (2006) 433–57.

Tick, Edward. *War and the Soul: Healing Our Nation's Veterans from Post-Traumatic Stress Disorder*. Wheaton, IL: Quest, 2005.

Tyler, Tom R. *Why People Obey the Law*. New Haven: Yale University Press, 1990.

United Nations General Assembly. *Basic Principles and Guidelines on the Right to a Remedy and Reparation for Victims of Gross Violations of International Human Rights Law and Serious Violations of International Humanitarian Law*. 2005. http://www.ohchr.org/EN/ProfessionalInterest/Pages/RemedyAndReparation.aspx.

United States Catholic Conference of Bishops. *Charter for the Protection of Children and Young People*. June 2002. http://www.usccb.org/issues-and-action/child-and-youth-protection/charter.cfm.

———. "A Community Response to Crime." *Origins* 7 (1978) 593–604.

———. *Responsibility, Rehabilitation, and Restoration: A Catholic Perspective on Crime and Criminal Justice*. Washington, DC: United States Catholic Conference, 2000.

Van Ness, Daniel. "Restorative Justice in Prisons." Prison Fellowship International Session 204. http://restorativejustice.org/am-site/media/restorative-justice-in-prison.pdf.

Verdeja, Ernesto. "A Normative Theory of Reparations in Transitional Democracies." *Metaphilosophy* 37 (2006) 449–68.

Verkamp, Bernard Joseph. *The Moral Treatment of Returning Warriors in Early Medieval and Modern Times*. Scranton: University of Scranton Press, 1993.

Vitoria, Francisco de. *Political Writings*. Edited by Anthony Pagden and Jeremy Lawrance. Cambridge: Cambridge University Press, 1992.

Volf, Miroslav. *The End of Memory: Remembering Rightly in a Violent World*. Grand Rapids: Eerdmans, 2006.

———. *Free of Charge: Giving and Forgiving in a Culture Stripped of Grace*. Grand Rapids: Zondervan, 2005.

Waldron, Jeremy. "Superseding Historical Injustice." *Ethics* 103 (1992) 4–28.

Walker, Margaret Urban. *Moral Repair: Reconstructing Moral Relations after Wrongdoing*. New York: Cambridge University Press, 2006.

———. *What Is Reparative Justice?* Milwaukee: Marquette University Press, 2010.

Weil, Simone. *Simone Weil: An Anthology*. Edited by Siân Miles. New York: Grove, 2000.

Whitmore, Todd. "Bridging Jesus' Missions to the Poor and the Wicked: Contributions from Attention to Culture." In *Violence, Transformation, and the Sacred: "They Shall Be Called Children of God"*, edited by Margaret R. Pfeil and Tobias L. Winright, 193–209. Maryknoll, NY: Orbis, 2012.

———. "Catholic Social Teaching: Starting with the Common Good." In *Living the Catholic Social Tradition: Cases and Commentary*, edited by Kathleen Maas Weigert and Alexia K. Kelley, 59–85. Lanham, MD: Rowman & Littlefield, 2005.

Wilson, William Julius. *When Work Disappears: The World of the New Urban Poor*. New York: Knopf, 1996.

Wolterstorff, Nicholas. *Justice in Love*. Grand Rapids: Eerdmans, 2011.

Wright, N. T. *Evil and the Justice of God*. Downers Grove, IL: InterVarsity, 2006.

———. *Scripture and the Authority of God: How to Read the Bible Today*. New York: HarperOne, 2013.

Zehr, Howard. *Changing Lenses: A New Focus for Crime and Justice*. Scottdale, PA: Herald, 1990.

CPSIA information can be obtained
at www.ICGtesting.com
Printed in the USA
LVOW08*1458191216

517949LV00005B/114/P